HARD-WIRED TO LEAD

Women's Leadership Context, Culture and Re-Construction

Hard-Wired to Lead
Copyright

Hard-Wired to Lead: The Culture of Silence and Women's Leadership

Hard-Wired to Lead. Volume 2. The Leadership Culture

Cover design by Okomota

Carmel Connections Inc. www.drcarmelananton.com

ISBN: 978-0-9862111-5-7

Series Title: Hard-Wired to Lead: Women's Leadership Context, Culture and ReConstruction

PRINTED IN THE UNITED STATES OF AMERICA

All biblical references are taken from the New International Version (NIV, 2001).
A comprehensive Bibliography for those interested in further reading, research and scholarship is provided, along with a short list of immediate resources to empower those who may feel they have no recourse.

VOLUME II: Leadership Culture

HARD-WIRED TO LEAD

The Culture of Silence and Women's Leadership

Table of Contents

Acknowledgments

To my husband love of my life and untiring supporter, thank you for believing in me and standing by me. To my children and family this project is for you.

To all who had a part in making this project a success

To my bae Rachel S. for your attention to detail, a special thank you.

To leaders who aspire to conscious, next-level leadership excellence

To Truth and Possibility - only when we acknowledge the Truth of a situation can we unlock limitless Possibility for growth and change.

To all who are Hard-wired to Lead

Your leadership matters. Find your hard-wire and lead.

Hard-Wired to Lead

The odds are against them
The voices will clamor
Intelligent, qualified but still
Inequitable honor
Against the grain they press
Wearing glamour, pants, or dress
Destined; hard-wired to lead

Re-writing social scripts
Re-shaping gendered roles
Following their hearts' calling
Like a River or the Sea, pounding
Despite rocks or shoals, and even falling
Relentless, persistent, passionate, abounding
Indeed! Called. Hard-wired to lead

Can't change their nature
Nor can stop their rise
Though often hindered, still they seek the prize
Scaling hurdles; Transcending Barriers

Embracing what they bring
Accepting that they are.
Stretching food or dollar
Yet people still follow
Those hard-wired to lead.

Revolutionary the influence
Shifting prevailing paradigms
Inevitable, Unstoppable Sea change
Sustaining the next generation
with transformative revelation
Of future personal possibilities
For all who are hard-wired to lead

Visionary Power
Fluid Execution
Charting the course
Opening Doors
With Purposive action
Pioneer or Blaze a Path
Creating novel Futures
Women. Hard-Wired to Lead

PROLOGUE

Misha was always considered to be bossy. She was filled with a burning curiosity, knew exactly where she wanted everything to be and what everyone needed to do. She sat in the front of the bus and could not understand why she couldn't. In fourth grade, she organized a block party and circus for her neighborhood, raising funds from those who attended. In fourth grade, she was left in charge of her classroom as the teacher stepped outside for a moment. She subsequently led in the student council, and became president of her sorority. Her Hard-wire to lead was evident across her life and has evolved into developing other leaders. She learned that other's perceptions of her skills and gifts may not be accurate or may be misunderstood. There is a profound often inexplicable societal and cultural resistance to women who lead in all sectors of life; however, this resistance is hidden behind a culture of silence in a patriarchal society. Often people see women's aspiration to lead and leadership as problematic, rather than acknowledging that the system itself, which excludes a large segment of the population is the problem.

This book is the second of three volumes in the *Hard-wired to Lead* women's leadership series. Each volume begins with a poem which summarizes the issues covered. This volume begins the discussion with chapter 8, which describes the 'hard-wired to lead' concept in women.

The concept of the 'hard-wire to lead' is a personal imprint embedded in our souls like a microchip or a preprogrammed hard-wire which is expressed differently depending on the unique calling, or 'the wiring' of the woman. Its actualization may be fostered or hindered based on access and opportunity in various environments and whether those around her celebrate it or negate it. Despite women's tendency to negate the hard-wire instinct, the hard -wire 'micro-chip' is always there. People do not always consider a woman's innate hard-wire or individual programming to be important, so it is frequently dismissed. These women would tend to be silenced. I believe the dismissal is because women are still socialized -some would argue created- to be homemakers, someone's assistant or best in supporting positions not in leading positions. It is this precise nexus that Chapter 9 explores in a practical, open and honest way what the 'code of silence' is, how it operates and what can be done to break it once it is identified.

Then, to debunk the persistent cultural perceptions and narratives to the contrary, in Chapter 10, the truth about women's leadership effectiveness is outlined.[1] Supported by research data, despite the barriers described in Volume 1, I set the record straight regarding women's leadership. This is followed by identifying three critical but persistent underlying societal narratives which continue to inform the responses and descriptions of women's leadership. These narratives are outlined as 'shades of truth' in Chapter 11, because they frame the thinking and perceptions of women's capability and competence in leadership, though many people are unable to articulate them. As the title implicates not all of the narratives perceptions are true, and some are only partially true from a post-modern perspective.[2] Chapter 12 examines attempts to explain the current understandings of women's quest to access leadership roles by presenting metaphors which help to quickly understand what might be happening in the context as a result of the workplace systems that hinder realization of women's leadership aspirations.[3] Some are familiar, and some are not.

Although I do not have an affiliation to any political party, I do mean for this book to highlight the recruitment and selection process of a woman candidate to a top leadership position for the very first time. To illustrate the challenges faced, the fundamental perceptual change needed, and the obvious effect on the collective consciousness of America in the aftermath I include a case study of the presidential race in Chapter 13. The way this national interview for the top leadership position in the nation was conducted created a riveting context and public illustration of the many covert barriers to leadership women face as described in the first volume. The case example further shows aspects of the culture of silence and the confusing narratives that are detailed in this volume. For the first time in our nation's history a woman became a major party nominee for president and the public experience became a striking and valuable illustration of contemporary leadership decision making and practice. I use it as a way to help us consciously grasp that what happened in public can mirror what often happens behind the closed doors of executive offices and within the search team or search firm deliberations when selecting a women candidate for leadership positions. The topic of women in leadership is a powerful one at this time because we are living in a pivotal, compelling, embodied revolutionary moment in our nation's history that challenges social consciousness and global maturity as we navigate the expanding landscape of women's leadership.

The 2016 presidential election was a visceral and emotional public experience which not only served to engage the nation in divisive conflict but sparked crucial leadership dialogues. Whether the nation can focus long enough to engage and bring the issues to a level of consciousness that produces action remains to be seen. A dangerous complacent paralysis with the status quo seems to have a stranglehold on those who currently are in power and sets up the issue of leaders' ethics and moral decision-making failures. The case carries the weight of what this volume seeks to illustrate about women and leadership: 1) the painful cost and consequences that can result from being capable and ready to lead when people are not prepared for, or accepting of, your leadership, 2) the power of persistent narratives that shape and guides public perception and response to a woman leader which may or may not be true, 3) the double-standard of expectations that women must transcend to access leadership opportunity in contrast to their male counterparts, and 4) how prevailing systems can negatively, and consequentially, influence leadership decisions. Chapter 14 concludes with a call and a charge for women to honor their hard-wire-to-lead aspirations.

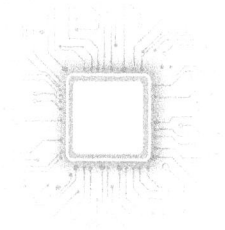

CHAPTER 8

HARD-WIRED: The Leadership Factor

"Don't let being a woman hold you back from the leader that you're destined to be"_ J. Farsnel

Women bring talent, experience, and education to their brand of leadership. Despite that fact, we do not see them represented in the top leadership positions. Organizations ordinarily aggressively vie with each other to recruit and promote talented experienced and educationally prepared candidates. However, whether we are talking about countries, Fortune 500 companies, governments, healthcare, finance or other service industries, there is clear evidence of a real and persistent disconnect between the clear qualifications (educational preparation, workforce presence, and managerial experience) of women and the presence of women as executive leaders.[1,2]

In the *Fifth Discipline*, Senge points out that women leaders are "people who do not come from the traditional centers of power but from the cultural, economic and demographic periphery,"[3] so, they can immediately engender fear, mistrust and unfavorable judgments by others who may be unconsciously predisposed to disqualify top women candidates from being recruited, promoted, or selected for top leadership positions.

Leadership is relational. My definition of leadership is that it is an influential relationship between a leader and follower established [or chosen] to achieve mutual goals.[4] Women do have influential power. However, when they exercise such power it frequently creates a disruptive effect that can make men feel threatened or trigger the desire to silence and control women. This translates into active resistance to women's operating in positions of power. So, women, as leaders, even as they create new possibilities for organization growth and competitiveness also increase the level of complexity across all dimensions and perceptions of leadership as we know it today. Research shows that traditional leadership theory is based on a male profile.[5] What happens, however when women display the agentic traits and characteristics traditionally associated with leadership theory? For some the response is perfectly normal. For other women the response is unthinkable because they are not male and are perceived to be out of place. It also can mean that women's leadership characteristics were not originally included in the repertoire of leadership characteristics. Data confirms that aspiring women leaders also continue to present a challenge to organizational search committees as the ongoing underrepresentation of women in chief or executive (C-level) level positions suggests.[2]

Organizations and nations continue to struggle with accepting women as leaders so we will begin by exploring why there is a struggle. Some of the questions that will be dealt with and supported by research and experience include: Are women competent and capable leaders? Do they have the leadership characteristics at all? What are the challenges in the leadership environment for women? Why are women so persistently underrepresented? What is the code of silence and why does it exist?

Is it that women just don't aspire to these positions? Is there a way that this dilemma can be resolved? These are just some of the overarching questions that will be addressed throughout this book. In this chapter the focus will be on the decision to choose women as leaders, and women's hard-wire to lead.

Making the Decision to Choose Women Leaders

The average business environment still is not ready for women's leadership. The data that only 5% of women hold top leadership positions attests to this. The decision to promote and place women in top leadership positions is influenced by a variety of factors. These factors include 1) company needs and the candidate's skill-set match, 2) society, culture and organization context, 3) the way women are generally perceived, 4) the lenses through which women's performance are evaluated, 5) the entrenched systemic barriers that frame the workplace environment, and 6) the traditional decision heuristic -or method and framework -of decision making practice.

How that decision is made speaks directly to the under-representation of women in the highest leadership positions. The decision is one that is fraught with challenges for the implicated women and for the decision makers. There are decision-making, societal, and ethical implications for the people involved. Two important notes are to be considered here. First, the importance of recognizing that even when decision makers are looking to make an objective choice, that choice is guided by core traditions, culture, beliefs, and biases unless there is purposive and intentional action to move beyond them. Second, the core traditions, culture, beliefs and biases form a framework or lens that serves as a deeply ingrained and unconscious 'cultural force' or filter that is a powerful driver of behavior, the selection process and the perception of who can be leaders.[5]

On culture, for example, Radford suggests that the importance and the complexity of a decision positively correlates to the amount of attention paid to finding a satisfactory solution, and that individual decision making may vary as a function of culture, asserting that: "any consideration of decision making behavior (or any behavior for that matter) needs to be considered in relation to the culturally accepted patterns of behavior of the particular society in which the decision is being made."[6] This means that there may be less consideration and importance (value) placed on choosing a woman to lead, simply because the culturally accepted patterns of a patriarchal society would not ordinarily be predisposed to selecting a woman over a man to lead. First because men are usually the decision makers, though women also operate from this pattern; second the traditional cultural patterns of leadership practice would be disrupted; and Lastly, it is usually easier to rationalize or justify a non-selection based on tradition or on something that the woman has done wrong, than to shape new patterns of thinking, deciding and behaving.

Singer further writes about culture as "a pattern of perceptions, values, attitudes and behaviors that is accepted and expected by an identity group", and that "each identity group has its own pattern of behavioral norms" and that individuals "must inevitably be a member of a myriad of different perceptual and identity groups simultaneously." [7] So the decisions made are influenced by the identity group or groups that one belongs to. Thus, your gender, age group, religious group, and culture can influence perspectives and expectations for appropriate roles.

Culture also influences perceptions and what are the appropriate behavior patterns – and roles – a person can hold. So, culture becomes a critical but often overlooked factor which affects decision making[8] and is strong enough to influence thought processes, perceptions, the individual's values, and the interpretation of information. The power of culture's influence also speaks to why women will vote against another woman or select a man with lesser qualifications or competencies over a woman for leadership positions -almost instinctively or because of tradition. Arguably, this cultural force could be at the heart of the seemingly immovable 4-5% number of women in top leadership positions and the incredibly difficult time women have in securing those positions even though they are fully qualified. I would acknowledge that half a century ago there may not have been enough women in the C-level talent pool. However, today that is no longer a valid argument, nor is it any longer a reason for the persistent underrepresentation of women in the top leadership positions. The next generation of women leaders is prepared and ready but leadership decision-making has not responded to women's preparedness and leadership ability as would be expected. The disconnect between readiness and the corporate and societal response is critical as we look at the leadership factor in women and how society and companies react to women who have it throughout the rest of this volume.

The Hard-Wire to Lead as a Leadership Factor

Many women are hard-wired to lead. Being born with the leadership factor means that leadership qualities and characteristics are innate or permanently wired into the personality and or psyche, such that it is not easily changed. The Hard-wire is different and unique to each woman, her destiny and the contribution she has been born to make in the world. Her gifting can be seen in government, education, finance, the arts, engineering, science, politics, media and entrepreneurship to name a few. Each leader has different talents, knowledge bases, capacities and frames of reference which are programmed into them to some extent. The hard-wire is a predisposition that draws the woman or influences her behavior, fuels their passions or governs the interests that they gravitate toward. Ultimately, the hard-wire honors their intellectual aptitude and affords natural facility for influence, advocacy, innovation in systems or transformation organizations, communities, and nations. As the title of the series suggests women's hard-wire to lead is a central argument of this Volume.

To be hard-wired in a broad or general sense is to be connected, as with electronic components, by electrical wires or cables…to implement a capability [or in this context a destiny] through logic circuitry that is permanently connected within a computer and therefore not subject to change by programming.[9] Leadership is in them. The hard-wire can also mean that the individual is pre-programmed as with a microchip with an information database that prescribes their optimal functional utility. The microchip or circuit board as metaphoric illustrations are used to highlight the real consequences of the barriers presented in volume one. What I mean in terms of leadership is that the women can be wired with innate life-logic capabilities, characteristics, and capacities to fulfill a destiny to lead. I would also argue that the intent or motivation for the behaviors that present barriers to women who want to lead are designed to change, hinder or limit any leadership potential in women. The logic of circuitry is so permanent that it is not subject to change whether home, community, society, or workplace are accepting of her 'wiring' or not: It will show up wherever the woman goes.

This tendency toward leadership can be evident early on to observers and it is either recognized facilitated and guided or stifled, tangled or re-wired (steered away in another direction), and spoken about as a negative characteristic. For young girls, especially, this can be problematic. The use of such words as bossy, out of line, and obstinate for example paint her innate leadership characteristics in a negative light, as opposed to the perception that is created when words such as leader, adventurous, gifted, or determined are used to describe the same characteristics.

This also begins the development of a path of silencing, hiding or shrinking away from who the girl really is and that can be quite difficult and challenging (a twisting or attempt at re-programming) for women who aspire to lead. A path that can result in women's low self-esteem, under-performance, a personal de-valuing and underrating of who they are by nature. There is also the constant tension between who others say they should be based on gender and who they know they really are. It is no wonder that a relevant study sought to identify what happened to girls' dreams of being leaders. Fels[10] studied whether women had abandoned their dreams of leadership. Somehow the dream seems to disappear for many girls along the way to maturity and the aspiration for advancement in the workplace or action on the aspirations seemed to vanish. Fels found that in environments where the woman is affirmed... The discussion on barriers in Volume I speaks to the overt tampering with this hard-wire as a phenomenon in society.

It is fascinating to watch parents push boys to be leaders and girls to be followers when either sex has the capacity to lead. Such parent behavior limits their daughter's leadership qualities early on. It is equally intriguing to see parents accept their children's hard-wire, and work to nurture, guide and develop it into full maturity. We admire this commitment to athletics when parents identify their child's 'gift' early on and are willing to sacrifice, move, or even mortgage their homes to give their child the best possible opportunity. Why is it not the same when it comes to girls' leadership gifts and characteristics? In fact, it can be quite difficult for the girl-child who has family and society stacked against her, whose characteristics create annoyance and anger rather than foresight and facilitation. Nonetheless, the hard-wire remains and will show up wherever there is a chance or opportunity to demonstrate it. Regina Kananji, a Malawian community leader stated it quite simply in response to an interview question: 'women are natural leaders.' I am pretty sure that there was no conversation with Geraldine Ferraro, the first female Vice-Presidential candidate nominee for a major party ticket who stated: "some leaders are born women".

If women recognize that they can lead, perhaps the quote which more aptly fits the situation is Kehler's statement: "If women would realize the influence they have, they would be filled with pride. If men recognized how influential women are, they would be scared to death."[11] Could it be that the fear of not being in control is what is keeping men from selecting qualified women to top leadership positions? It is possible that men do realize the extensive influence that women have and are strategic in the crafting of the narrative and the systems in place to ensure that their fears are allayed by excluding women from leadership opportunities. It is also possible that women do not clearly realize the influence they have, and so are taken advantage of such systems. I believe the crucial link lies in how men have learned from families that for them leadership characteristics are acceptable but not for women. Also, the patriarchal culture and society reinforces and frames leadership and other key agentic behaviors as suitable for boys versus not girls. We address this in the chapters that follow from the woman's perspective, but the situation is both thought-provoking and problematic and adds to the complexity of what will be the focused content of this volume where we go behind the context to understand the workplace culture that lies beneath the barriers. Understanding the context, beliefs, socializations and behaviors undergirding the leadership context that contributes to the under-representation of women in top leadership positions is vital.

The woman who is hard-wired to lead must figure out a way to deal with and live with this inner force throughout her lifetime. Leadership is a gift that is connected to destiny. The hard-wire becomes a persistent drive that shows up in the unusual places that call the gift out in the person. The hard-wire to lead is evident in girls and women who take charge or keep a cool head in emergencies, in the women others tend to look to for answers, in the young ladies who are 'found' by leadership, and in female employees whose leadership showed up frequently enough for them to stand out from the rest just as 'cream rises to the top' these women grab attention.

Before I spend further time on the leadership aspect it is important as you read further for there to be recognition that everyone is a unique one-of-a-kind original. The mold by which you were made was thrown away, and there is no one like you in the world! This means that what you are gifted and wired to do is your unique personal assignment. No other person can ever fulfil your destiny or purpose quite like you. The need to compare yourself to other people, or the feelings of inadequacy – once you find your niche and are operating in it should be eliminated. Again, it also confirms that you have unique combination of strengths that can be developed and honed through learning and leadership experiences.

Your personality and the skills you inherently possess, also considered your 'gifts', reflect how you are 'wired'. It is a sort of map to your purpose here on earth. While I know that leadership skills and concepts can be taught and developed, as I have done the last two decades, there is something about people and women that are hard-wired to lead. It means that wherever these women are, even if they did not intend to, they end up leading in groups, teams, organizations and the world. The uniqueness is borne out in all the various sectors, disciplines, professions and positions that women lead in from finance to politics to sports to name a few. The tendency toward leadership is innately and integratively available for development and actualization because of the built in hard-wire. As with life, one of the critical issues will always be the environmental context that the individual is in, as it makes a difference in whether the individual abandons the hard-wire or thrives and operates fully in their gift. One of this volume's goals is to identify and decode some of the hidden environmental factors that create challenges for women who lead, in ways that their male counterparts do not experience.

Personal Hard-wire

My hard-wire includes leadership decades of leadership, translating ideas into systems, departments, programs and company start-ups, and identifying bias, developing inclusion strategies and advocating for those who were discriminated against or treated unfairly. I cut my leadership teeth in my early teens as leader of an AWANA[12] team (acronym for Approved Workmen Are Not Ashamed). Each community youth program has a director and uses team games, behavioral discipline and scripture memorization to 'reach kids, equip leaders and change the world for God." I learned to develop creative unconventional ways to come up with wins, even though all the best players were already selected. My team won many of the weekly competitions with the odds were stacked against us -age, gender, experience, type of players. Our program, located in an urban primarily Hispanic community, ultimately won the national Olympics in all categories. Ultimately, I introduced and replicated the program in another urban location in a primarily Black community. I led several City summer programs which pushed my creativity and innovation capacity as a young leader. I added resilience and management skills to my leadership repertoire as co-founder and co-director of the Ambassadors, a 40-member music and drama group that traveled to perform.

Some of the leadership positions I applied for as with the city summer program. Others I was invited, or I proposed like the program I replicated. In all the early leadership contexts, women were not allowed to lead on their own. The two methods of leadership available to me were leading as co-director and leading from behind a male director that I had trained. These leadership opportunities were the 'formal' leadership positions I could hold as a woman, particularly in the context of the church. I subsequently lead or was recruited to lead across different sectors in for profit, state, and government entities with increasing levels of budgets over a million dollars and personnel responsibility. I have started up departments and award-winning revenue-generating community programs from scratch, taught, developed and coached leaders and aspiring leaders, and facilitated spiritual transformations through ministry. Each of the environments in which I worked either fostered and facilitated my hard-wire to lead, or were hostile seeking to stifle, rewire, and limit it to fit the perception of what others thought my hard-wire needed to be.

In Volume 1, the chapters focus on power secrets and women's leadership and looks at contextual barriers based on image, gender, sex, money, and the church. Those chapters describe graphic women's experiences as they operate in leadership and in the work context.

Together with the chapter on ethics they shed light on the culture that shapes the context and some of the discriminatory behavioral systems against women in organizations in a way that leadership authors have not always included as part of the leadership discourse. At the end of the day, my leadership has brought increased revenue to the companies for which I worked, and I have had the wonderful privilege of shaping and impacting thousands of lives through teaching, speaking, training, coaching, and development of people and systems. As a pragmatist, even in those places where my contributions and potential were not fully understood or appreciated, there was a recognition of my leadership as vitally important. Women make up more than 50% of the workplace employees and the population. Their presence in the workplace has reached critical mass, where women's presence can no longer be ignored. As a result the absence of women's representation in leadership positions is of fundamental significance to societal, business, economic and national, and global growth and well-being well into the 21st century and beyond.

Times have changed in relation to the response to women's leadership. There used to be a reflexive negative response triggered to just the thought of a woman leading. While the negative responses have not all gone, the current *zeitgeist* (spirit or mood of this particular period in history) has shifted in two major ways as shown by the ideas and beliefs of these time. First, our culture and society has increasingly become more open to women leaders. Second, women are no longer as silent as they used to be about their experiences and capabilities. There is an awakening as women realize the power of their voices and the capacity for leading. Although women still remain significantly under-represented in leadership positions and there is still strong resistance to women leaders in some sectors, there continues to be increasing awareness of the value and economic impact as a population group. The irony of such a reflexive negative response and the resilient persistence required by women to combat it was not lost on me. I shared in Volume 1 that the first conscious observation of such women's leadership in action was from the first female leadership role model I had: My mother. Here is some of what I learned about leadership through observing her, from personal experience and from observing what other women have done as they go about the responsibilities of motherhood. As I identify the leadership skills that motherhood draws from the women, the term 'leader-moms' will be used. The term 'Leader-Moms' describes how the skills of the leader integrate with the responsibilities of motherhood. The term also serves to illustrate other realities such as the mother being a leader in her home, she can also simultaneously be the leader in her company, and she could have birthed a leader-child.

My mother embodied the term 'Leader-Mom.' She was a Nurse-Midwife by profession who became a stay at home mother. When we were children, she had help with some of the household duties but managed the bulk of the responsibilities with my father. There were seven of us. She ultimately held leadership positions in the church, the community and in the workplace as Nurse Manager. Mothers are natural leaders in a context that has unique challenges. Unlike contemporary companies, there is no human resources department, no previous recommendations, resumes or historical behavioral patterns from which to select for their preferred child. Mothers have no control over the personality each one of their children are born with. They may have one or several children. Sometimes, as in my case, there may be more than one child at the same time. There is no interview or selection committee. Beyond the sonogram outlines mothers would never have laid eyes on their children before birth. The assignment? To co-facilitate the growth and development of the human beings entrusted to their care. The goal? to help them reach adulthood. There is no script or instruction manual to go by or roadmap to manage the complexity of the assignment: except love, and the connection with the creator.

The children they are given responsibility for are also pre-wired with everything they need, yet still they are totally dependent on the mother and father. Mothers learn on the job as they interact as leaders and guides for their children. Whether working or staying at home, mothers must find a way to take care of and lead in the lives of their charges until the children are able to do so for themselves. I believe single parents are specially gifted and graced by their creator with extra capacity, and I respect the numerous responsibilities they must handle daily on their own. Many children as they grow are not initially aware of the sacrifices mothers make on their behalf. They mostly know that their needs are met; and that they mostly get what they ask for. Creativity and innovative situational leadership characteristics are modeled daily. I use the word model because children will imitate you faster than do what you ask or tell them to.

Here are some of the specific leadership characteristics that are evident in Leader-Moms:

i. Visionary – they envision a wonderful future of their children, based on the gifts they see in them; they learn to know and read their children from the early nuances of their cries; to what they like; to what they need. All is premised on the desire that their children's lives will be better than theirs. They patiently and protectively nurture and sacrifice for years to bring that vision into fruition.

ii. Strategic – These women develop and execute very complex systems strategies as they go about managing their children's scheduled activities along with their own. Managing the daily activities, always with the future of that child, the unique needs, their gifts and the family collective in mind.

iii. Socially and emotionally intelligent – such intelligence is evident as these women broker, negotiate, resolve conflict, read and mitigate emotional distress, and advocate for their children bridging the interface of myriad relationships on their behalf. There is the ability to pick up when children are sick or upset and the wisdom to take care of them and calm them down. The social intelligence is evident in the harmony and smooth functioning of their home, where they operate as peace-makers when there is conflict, and in the interest of fairness.

iv. Decision-makers - they are creative, insightful and incisive decision makers. As productivity and resource masters considering all that is accomplished or done in one day. They can stretch not just food, but dollars too. They can patch (and fix) just about anything -from cuts, to toys, and even broken hearts.

v. Creators- they are a constant fountain of ideas for activities and creative possibilities with answers to the myriad questions children have. Operating as prolific and persistent problem solvers, as initiators of alternative ways and means to stretch food and dollar as they successfully manage a revolving budget, these women are highly integrative innovators. Sometimes these activities are engaged simultaneously.

vi. Nurturers -they recognize the needs and potential in their children; then as developers they will support, coach, cajole, encourage, challenge, promote, vigorously applaud and reward the accomplishments of their children. These behaviors can be ongoing throughout the life of the child to reinforce their identity when the socio-cultural, educational and workplace environments present negative information or seek to change the individual's natural hard-wire.

vii. Connected multi-taskers- leader-moms manage the emotional, relational, psychological, oh yes, and physical needs of their families, maintaining the harmony between individuals in their households while striking a delicate balance between being chief comforter and chief disciplinarian.

viii. Loyal -almost to a fault: Leader-Mom's are the greatest fan, first and staunchest supporters and are often the last remaining supporter when everyone else has gone. So dependable that they are known to come through for their children over and over again -yes, even when it may be undeserved.

ix. Servant Leaders - Mothers serve first; selflessly ensuring that the needs of their loved ones are met. Quite often the result is that their needs are pushed to the back-burner or, sometimes, never met at all.

x. Unconditional - in their enduring love and commitment is not transactional; their tenacious faith; and persistent prayer in seeing to the spiritual development of their charges.

Leader-moms display authentic, transformational, 'servant' leader qualities. As a society we have come to expect these leader-mom characteristics and take them for granted or as a given or expectation celebrating them one day out of the year with dinner, rest, cards, and thank-yous. Some mothers still must continue just like they do every other day of the year because there is no one else to relieve her from this leadership responsibility even on her special day. Mothers are unpaid for tireless labor.[13] What if mothers only led or worked one day out of the year? What would happen on the remaining days at home, in schools, in the workplace?

Well the reverse approach was tried in 2017 on the March 8 International Women's Day celebration which was also to be designated as 'A Day without a Woman.'[13] It was to be a day when women took a day off from work (or went on strike) and marched or protested so that the impact of their presence in the workplace could be felt and recognized in terms of labor and consumer power, value and contribution. Many participated in the walk out and gathered with others who were like-minded and similarly fortunate. Some critics argued that those who were able to walk out were privileged.[14] I used the word fortunate because some women knew that they would place their jobs in jeopardy or become marked by participating. Others who needed the income or who for health or other reasons could not participate -for even that day- may have faced a choice simple enough for them: march or lose the job. March or not pay rent. What is important here is that while individuals may have a clear understanding of history and want to participate, there is also a clear understanding of the existential reality, which prevents them from doing so. Some women stayed on the job because they had to, working in potentially difficult work environments, perhaps being in a situation where they would have no job to return to the next day. Even wearing red in solidarity to work could become a flag in organizations where the culture does not appreciate such behavior making the woman-in-red a target for retaliation, barriers, and challenges because she would have unwittingly activated the codes in place that are strengthened by silencing anyone who has the desire to speak out on equity. So, that 'Day Without a Woman' protest generated mixed reactions from schools that had to close for the day, to companies that offered perks to female customers. This highlights one of the challenge-layers of women in the workplace: perks and days off may be granted, but the most important thing needed, the Equal Rights Amendment (ERA),[15] continues to be withheld from women and contributes to persistent company culture and bias.

The Hard-Wire and Leadership Practice

Most people would agree that women are the lynch pins of most organizations as middle managers, administrative and executive assistants, secretaries and sometimes CEO's. The majority of them work at low to middle level positions in the organization. It is their mostly supportive leading roles that make the company run smoothly. Women's roles in companies quite often are crucial to company survival, just as it is known that their leadership role is vital for the survival of the family. However, there seems to be a deeper problem and issue at work when women's knowledge, skills, and abilities are available to a capitalistic society, but because of culture and traditional mindsets the prevalent and lucrative opportunity of their leadership and competitive revenue generation are disregarded.

The disconnect is clearly evidenced through women's lack of representation in the C-Suite and the research that shows they are prepared and capable. Another disconnect is outlined in Chapter ten on the perception of women's leadership effectiveness, where the truth is that corporations still 'penalize' women based on gender in terms of their work evaluations or when they return from maternity leave. This alone can cause salaries to take a huge hit at just the time it is most needed. Such companies are also disregarding the fact that motherhood contributes to developing, honing and refining the very leadership skills that are truly needed in the workplace. Women lose their upward trajectory when they step away from the workplace to raise a young family; or, work expectations become unreasonable when critical activities (such as meetings; networking events) are set at hours that women may be responsible for dropping off or picking up their children. Such hours may work well for their male counterparts because they have a wife or partner to take care of these extraneous or extra-curricular responsibilities for them. Women in the workplace *are* the wife; the mother; and the leader. The number of women in the workplace has steadily increased to numbers that can no longer go unheeded. These women are leaders, and their leadership abilities and capacities can no longer be controlled away. In other words, I argue in this volume that the conditions some women work under are conditions that border on – or are downright examples of- controlling abusive behavior. Yet these issues and many others remain 'undiscussables' in the workplace despite the presence of laws to the contrary because of the code of silence. The difficulty lies in that much of what happens is shrouded by a culture of silence which is invisible, intractable, and powerful.

The implication here for leaders is the importance of thinking beyond the leadership status quo. Leadership practice can strategically and consciously ensure that the work environment becomes ergonomically re-standardized to include women at all levels. Ergonomic disconnects are seen in basic things such as uniform sizes, equipment standard measures, microwave and cabinet height levels, private showers, cockpit sizes, truck and bus seats where instruments are not appropriately sized. Companies can implement or change these things to communicate that women are accepted and welcome, rather than continuing to expect women to silently endure or adapt to an uncomfortable environment. Not all do so. I believe these and other issues need to be part of all leadership workplace environment and safety assessments and should be included in Human Resources department ergonomic initiatives. These are not top of mind if women are not at the evaluation and decision-making levels. If women are a part of the workforce, an equitable workplace needs to reflect that at all levels. An example of fundamental workplace gender bias was recently brought to national attention with the NASA historic women-only spacewalk that did not happen.[16] The alleged issue? The size of the uniform available for one of the women. Her graciousness was admirable, but she and all the aspiring women and girls were ultimately cheated out of that history-making experiential accomplishment. The report is that the astronaut in question made the decision not to go and to allow a male counterpart to go in her place. A decision response that illustrates the complex conundrum that any person who operates in a discriminatory environment clearly understands. A decision that was gracious, didn't rock the boat but which nevertheless forced her to choose between living her dream and succumbing to inherent gender bias. The report further indicates that it was easier to switch out people than to make a uniform that fit. Hmmm. My question is why was this not considered important enough to be addressed ahead of time since the uniform size and planned walk situation was well known? This experience is replicated across many industries and goes beyond just the building and equipment levels to include things like room temperature, lack of lactation rooms beyond the bathroom, or childcare options.

At another level the economic disconnect of the wage gap continues to persist supported by a lack of corporate and legal accountability hidden by a lack of transparency. The negative consequences for women are life-long in terms of impact yet there is no will in the leadership culture to change to one where equality is proactive and expected rather than reactive and enforced. At another level, beneath the ongoing challenges faced by women in leadership cultures that may be unconsciously biased, hostile or abusive are the emotional and psychological challenges for women that result. These daily experiences call for a human-factors engineering.[17] initiative to make contemporary leadership culture one where women's interactions with their work environment are more efficient and prioritizes their safety, allowing them to craft a career trajectory that follows or honors their hard-wire to lead. Leadership culture has become inured with workplace policies and behavioral practices that have resulted in discrimination against women's and under-representation in leadership roles because they have opened the door to women but have not accepted them enough to make permanent accommodations that focuses on their well-being. It will take the social architecture of transformational leadership, and collaboration of all actors (leader, females and males) to effect needed change. The first step is to recognize the power inherent in the code of silence which adds to the complexity of workplace culture in relation to women. We don't talk about these issues nearly enough. When an incident makes us discuss and examine behaviors and practices there is a rush to explain it away, perhaps deal with that single issue rather than addressing the root problem, and it all fades away into the silence of inactivity -until the next incident. Silence will be the focus of attention in the upcoming chapter.

Précis

This reflective introduction looked at the hard-wire to lead, the unique wiring that can show up in women from an early age, some may have leader-mom models, others may not. The environmental context, and the response of people in that context can strengthen and nurture; or scramble and seek to re-wire the woman. Decisions to recognize or choose women as leaders are influenced by the culture and society in which they live. The culture and society can present barriers that contribute to the perpetuation of under-representation of women in top leadership positions despite their hard-wire. This has become tacit in the organization because of the code of silence; and will demand transformational leaders' social architecture to re-design a work environment ergonomically conducive to women's ability to honor their hard-wire to lead.

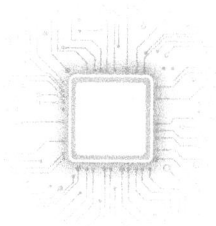

CHAPTER 9

The Code and Culture of Silence

*"No person is your friend who demands your silence or denies your right to grow."*_Alice Walker

Guns are deadly weapons. When the gun is fired, the pressure that is built behind the bullet propels it at high velocity to its target. The sound of the gunshot is made as the pressure is released at the opening of the gun.[1] The sound is distinct and recognizable, so when it is heard people drop to the ground or run for their safety. A unique and powerful optional feature of guns is that they have silencers. Silencers allow killers to do their deadly work, and even those who are close by may not be aware that a life was taken, because the telltale sound one would normally hear is missing or masked. Silencers work best if people or the environment conspire with the killer by contributing noise whether they are aware of it or not, at the time the deadly action is taking place. It is only afterward that the significance of what has occurred can be identified.

The statistics of women's leadership which show persistent under-representation of women in top leadership positions is surrounded by unique silence. Not many companies or leaders want to talk about women not being represented at top leadership levels. The data confirms that women are educationally prepared, have accrued undeniable professional experience and want to lead.[2] The body of research on the barriers and hurdles faced by women would not be as robust as it is today if women did not aspire to lead and had the fulfillment of their leadership aspirations denied. What then is preventing them from holding leadership positions in companies and sectors? I believe there is some mechanism in place that 'kills women off' from leadership positions before organizations, incumbent leaders or women can figure out, or identify, what has occurred. In companies, the deadly work is often completed with the silencers of privilege, the good old boys club, gender role expectations, organization barriers, lack of awareness and shame -to name just a few factors. So, because the action occurred behind a wall of silence the 'killers' can get away with the behavior, or at least it takes longer for the damage or the perpetrator to be noticed. Attention is drawn when observers notice that aggregate numbers are too small for too long to ignore and society or researchers notice the phenomenon and begin to ask questions. By then, the victims who could provide key evidence -or help with answers- are out of the picture, their voices silenced. In fact, the faster the victim can be removed, the longer the silence can be extended since related evidence would be removed. Let us examine what the Code of Silence is and how it is developed and maintained in workplace and societal culture. We will also look at the consequences of breaking the silence and coming to voice can mean for women and marginalized groups.

The Code of Silence

A code signals secrecy. Codes mean that something may be hidden in plain sight: it requires insider knowledge to be able to decipher the code, what it means, and how it can be applied. A code is a "system of a system of words, letters, behaviors or signs used to represent a message in secret form, or a system of numbers, letters, or signals used to represent something in a shorter or more convenient form" words.[3] Examples include our DNA code, computer codes, language codes, or codes to open a safe. Things such as behaviors, workplace practices, societal expectations are also written in cultural codes. Sometimes we know the code, other times we don't -it depends on whether we are in the in-group or inner circle of trust or not. Others can share the code with you or you can figure it out through observation, or stumble on it by mistake. In the show *It Takes a Thief*[4] the main character Alexander Mundy's hallmark was that he was expert at picking locks and deciphering intricate, top-secret codes with keen observation, an expert listening ear, and the sensitive touch of his hands.

In order to effectively operate in a coded system, one has to break, crack, decipher or receive the code. The greatest problem facing this work is that many would prefer that the code never be broken because this kind of culture works perfectly for them. The reason for code secrecy is to preserve a protective 'zone of silence' and lack of accountability that grants perpetrators the freedom to continue their misconduct. Silence is created by the forces of socialization, the narratives and role prescriptions of society and fear in the workplace culture. The silence is also about what would be uncovered if that silence were broken and how it would impact the ability to retain power and privilege as the right of only a certain few or ensure that barriers remain in place or can be further expanded. I found that the code of silence runs deeper, is stronger, and has a broader reach than I thought at first. Although society and culture operate by this code of silence, few can articulate it, and those who can, would rather not. There are just some things we don't want to talk about, and there are specific requirements for children, women, men, and leaders. Socialization begins early in life.

The Code of Silence in the Workplace and in Society

'Children should be seen and not heard.' Is the code being taught as children. Popular opinion wants women to be trophies, support their husband's career but have few opinions or careers of their own. Women are to look pretty on their arm, support the man, but have no voice. Then, there's the persistent undercurrent and mantra intoned to younger women, and sometimes explicitly 'taught' in churches and some academic contexts and supported by culture, the workplace and society: Women are to stay home and take care of the children. It is touted as 'the highest calling' though often undervalued in terms of the stated worth, and unpaid. The pressure is very real. The punishment for not honoring social role prescriptions is also real. The economic ramifications, such as discrimination and wage inequity, for refusing to be boxed into the role prescriptions is also very real. I've heard it joked about, or stated, in a sexist way that women should be kept barefoot and pregnant (ultimately silent in the public sphere) -as if that is all they are capable of. Some of these young women, who are exceptionally bright, forego their intellectual development (or honoring their hard-wire to lead), to try to stay at home, raise or take care of children -some ultimately never realizing their destiny or potential. What I am saying is that this role is not all that women are capable of. Just as not all women are called to lead, not all women are mothers. Women who are hard-wired to do more should be able to do more without guilt, shame, pressure or punishment.

I am not saying there is anything wrong with the decision to be a homemaker. That is, for young families where this is possible and for the woman who wants to do it. This leads me to raise two other factors which make this decision more complex than first meets the eye they are race and socioeconomic status. Many people see a difference between women of color and white women in terms of perception, response to their visibility, work performance, their leadership effectiveness even though both have challenges because of gender. Another significant difference also involves how race impacts socioeconomic status and how it has historically and contemporarily shaped the decision to stay at home for women of color and white women. Families of color are often two-career families which do not have the luxury of the woman staying at home because of low wages and status.[5] The spouse's income may not be high enough to singularly sustain their desired status. The disturbing distinctive of Black women is their historical involuntary and unpaid presence in the economy, where they historically supported, sometimes substituted for, the maternal role of the slave owner's wife as part of their duties. After abolition and emancipation, many later served as underpaid domestic servants and teachers. Though the contemporary economy has shifted somewhat with their increased presence in the workplace, women of color in the existing workplace are still underpaid, still disproportionately making up workers in the service, child-care and home-care industries where worker pay continues to be low and abuse and harassment high.[6] Schow would argue the reasons women are underpaid are myriad, and that women choose or gravitate to low paying positions, professions or industries that are low paying. Justification for pay inequity because they are 'not in demand'.[7] I argue that social mobility and access to better paying positions continues to be a challenge This also connects back to the conflict of patriarchal perception of privilege and understanding of how racial history continues to shape contemporary behavior as I mentioned in Chapter 8 in relation to the 'A

Day Off Work.' One of the reasons some women could not take the day off to strike, or even wear red in solidarity was because they were not in a position, or context where that was possible without being targeted or still retaining their jobs.

Another point I am making is that for women the result of the decision to stay home, even temporarily, frequently is the loss of ground in terms of socioeconomic status and in the company, loss of her 'place in line' for promotions. Current organization perceptions dismiss the leadership skills, or performance productivity before women take maternity leave and ascribe a negative attitude, value and worth of the home-maker role in society. Exactly as they are expected to behave by societal expectations. Yet, ironically, it is in this very private space where crucial leadership qualities are forged, developed, and refined as was highlighted in chapter eight. The salient issue is that there is little option for recognition or respect of the leader-mom skills honed in the home (the private space), much less the direct possibility of transferring them to the workplace (the public space). For some families of color, the decision to stay at home is often a luxury and a conundrum. The woman working outside the home can be a necessity if the family wants to live at a middle-income level. Or, she may be head of household or breadwinner. Women who stop out to raise a family tacitly make the choice to lose ground in their career advancement trajectory, and sometimes lose their position entirely.[8] Out of sight in the organization frequently means out of mind in terms of career advancement. These concepts culminate into the reality that women's voices are often not at the decision-making or sponsors table; their opinions are silenced; unrepresented in the public sphere because they are not there in enough leadership numbers to make a difference. So, the leadership gap persists. what is this code of silence as it pertains to women and leadership?

The Layers of Silence in Women's Leadership

As in the metaphor of the gun silencer that began this chapter, the organizational code of silence is similar in that its use reinforces and perpetuates organizational culture behavior. As with anything complex there are nuances or what I call layers of silence, representing the various forms and purposes of silencing. The lowest layer of silence paralyzes or reduces the pushback recoil that would ordinarily occur, so as more women fall victim, the likelihood of accuracy in targeting them increases and is reinforced. Silence further reduces the flash that would ordinarily shine a light on the disconfirming behaviors in contemporary leadership culture, making it more difficult to pinpoint who the person is erecting the barrier. Perpetrators can then operate under cover or in obscurity and not be held accountable for their actions. Additionally, there are oblivious male colleagues present, their bodies silently serving as the collegial 'solid objects' which create confusion in women on where the challenges or barriers originate. These silent colleagues add to the layer of difficulty women have in being able to identify who can/cannot be trusted. Leadership culture provides a perfectly chosen environment for sniper-like positioning of leader and or colleague to maintain the status quo. The sniper location can only be identified when the directional source of the shot can be pin-pointed. The irreconcilable differences between the numerical representation of female workers, documentation of women's capabilities or competence as leaders and the undeniable reality that they are severely underrepresented in the top leadership positions in virtually all sectors and walks of life. These factors constitute the significant and visible damage evidenced as the statistical scorecard of the company. It is the public layer of silence. Martin Luther King Jr. stated "there comes a time when silence is betrayal"[9] and I believe women have been betrayed by years and layers of silence. The various uses and purposes of silence gives leaders the ability to use it as a tool to facilitate and sustain organization practice. Next are some of the ways silence is used or exploited so it becomes bias against women in leadership practice.

Silence as a Broker in Leadership Practice

Silence is the powerful broker of the problematic interface of women's underrepresentation in leadership positions. As broker, silence blocks the women's ability to connect their individual experience to the broad societal problem. Women in such a position are marginalized and do not share with others about their experiences, so they believe they alone have the problem, not realizing that other women also have similar experiences. Silence guards faulty decision making, and supports unfair workplace practices. Silence colludes to cover abusive behavior, and falsely rationalizes disconfirmation. Silence helps to set traps, erect barriers, perpetuate blindness, and create hostages. Silence is a powerful entity. Its strength comes from cultural socialization that is deeply ingrained across generations, gender, and societal systems and structures. The silence of the privileged nurtures the silence of the oppressed. The privileged are silent to maintain their power and control advantage; the oppressed are silent for their protection and ability to function within the social systems and structures they must navigate.[10] Both types of silence need each other to coexist: the one to brush away or minimize the expressed need to come out of silence of the oppressed; and the other to be complicit in remaining silent for the systems and structures to operate smoothly and remain, so business can be conducted as usual. Voluntary change initiatives are scarce and reactive on the part of leaders and organizations. Laws have been needed to change the systemic structures over which silence has a stranglehold. However, the laws have been slow in coming and ineffective in achieving even basic changes. The code of silence is reflexive and resides deep in the cultural and individual subconscious. Its reach is wide and the connection to the power structure is strong. In fact, I believe that the structures of power cannot remain the same if the silence is broken and women, advocates, activists, sponsors and mentors alike engage in dialogue and collaborative action to weaken and break the silence -stranglehold. For some, this may be terrifying, but for others it signals new possibilities for growth, change, and maturity. Those who challenge the code are often punished (implicitly or explicitly) for disrupting the code and the status quo. But there are times when we can be silent no more; when code-breakers are required. Here, I hope to integrate the work experiences of women in the complex fabric of society, work and life, so that both women and men can recognize their part in the process of breaking the silence and collaboratively work towards the change that will benefit all and ultimately the bottom line.

The Currency of Silence in Leadership Practice

Brokers, serving as intermediaries, buy, sell or negotiate assets with some form of currency. Silence, as a broker, serves as an intermediary between the privileged and the oppressed. The privileged group in a patriarchal society wants to main power and control over other groups not considered to be in the privileged group. Women in business and leadership fall in the second category. The assets at stake include but are not limited to promotions, the work environment, opportunities for career advancement, perception of competency, decision making power, perception of image and leadership capability, worth and earnings, are brokered daily in leadership culture. The commission of this brokered relationship is the maintenance of silence and the withholding of privileges from the unprivileged group. This translates into billions of dollars annually, and over the lifetime of victims much more.

Specific assets in question are addressed in Volume 1 as specific barriers in relation to image, gender, sex, money and religious values. If you are still wondering what 'culture of silence' the book focuses on and why it needs to be broken, continue reading this unapologetic discussion of what lies behind the invisible barriers to women's access to top leadership positions. The narratives, rationalizations, biases, behaviors and even some of the consequential outcomes will be examined. The approach I take will be a binary approach, not because the complexity is not recognized but for contrast and for comparative clarity in the discussion. The layers of complexity will be woven in to complete the full picture for readers.

Partners in the Code of Silence

There are several partners that strengthen the power in the code of silence: fear, shame and guilt, perception of safety, abuse, systems awareness, and privilege. Collectively they serve as the means by which silence becomes difficult to break.

Fear and Silence. A major operating partner of silence is the fear that surrounds the collective experiences of women who lead in the workplace. The fear that speaking out will jeopardize their options for career advancement causes many to not share. The fear of being perceived as ungrateful for the opportunity granted them to lead, even though; even though that opportunity may be one that is rife with stress, undervaluation, and disrespect for their leadership styles keeps some silent. After all, these women have arrived in that coveted position of power and because they are so rare, they don't have many others to speak to who would understand their struggles and positional challenges, so there is hesitation in reaching out to others. So, they remain voiceless.

Shame and Silence. Though one can be prepared for it, there is still shame and embarrassment about expressing the reality of the leadership positions that many covet and aspire to hold. This ought not to be. To protect the executive image -women remain silent, ignore it or only focus on the opportunity. Does this sound in any way familiar? Or is this something that is totally new to you? Silence is also strengthened because of shame and guilt at what is happening to us. When we talk about experiences that are painful but recognized as the societal norm, it can be accepted at an unconscious level as 'just the way it is' and victims work harder to do their jobs or to find ways to survive in systems in which they are not designed to thrive, while silence retains control. The silence of victims here is self-protective or based on shame and wanting to be a team-player on a team that is harming or compromising her performance.

Perception of Safety and Silence. People keep silent for many reasons. It could be that as victims they were threatened with harm, coerced or convinced that by being silent they will be safe. Sounds like it might be true, at face value, but with the silence of bystanders the victim is further opened up to the danger of having harmful behavior repeated. Ultimately, as Audre Lorde points out "your silence will not protect you"[11] from my perspective it means that neither the silence of onlookers nor the silence of victims can predict or ensure victim safety. The problem? When there is silence there is also perceived complicity. The seeming agreement also perpetuates the very systems that oppress or harm the victims. bell hooks[12] confirms this aspect when she says that silence can be an act of complicity that serves to perpetuate prevalent ideas and I would add company culture and practices.

Silence could also mean that victims are consciously aware of the dominant culture and choose to be silent because it is less difficult or serves as temporary protection. So, whether the silence is believed to be strategic or not, it is complies with the dominant behavioral practices and it appears that the person has bought into or is in acceptance of the oppressive behavior. A position illustrated Parker Palmer with he said "for years, African Americans were silent in the presence of whites -silent, that is, about their true thoughts and feelings,… for years women were similarly silent in the presence of men."[13] Today, that silence continues partly in the workplace around the selection practices of many executive positions and search firms but is rapidly changing in society around the sexual harassment and wage inequity.

Systems Awareness and Silence. In silence, there appears to be agreement that what is occurring is acceptable -even though it may not be- we are sending the message that it is. Silence can also be because the woman may not be consciously aware of what is happening to them in the systemic structures of the environment. For example, if the society is unjust and unfair people "will be socialized across their lifespan to misunderstand their identity, needs, what constitutes happiness, what is good and of value and how one should act in one's relations."[14] Once a person is socialized to the system in society or in the workplace it reproduces itself in the people. Sometimes even though the system is against you, sets up barriers to hinder you, you can agree that the system's hindering you or oppressing you is acceptable, so you go along with it. I believe that individuals (and in this instance, women) also contribute to the perpetuation of systemic workplace practice. Palmer points out that dominance is perpetuated "when the socially powerful group convinces the other group that it is in their best interest to do what the [dominant group wants] them to do."[14] For example, the company's silent gatekeepers, women or men who decide against women or set them up for failure are mostly thinking that their contribution to the system will make them the exception to the rule of oppression as a result the culture of the organization remains undisclosed.[15]

The key here is the level of awareness and whether that consciousness-level is high enough to make women comfortable talking about it. Sometimes women just don't know -that's why I call it a code. Once women know, or have felt the sting of oppression's lash, the blow of being overlooked, and the crushing betrayal of being passed over for a male who is less qualified than they are, it becomes a difficult experience but one they may finally be able to talk about. Freire's concept of *conscientization*[16] in his radical educational model is perfectly suited for what is occurring in contemporary leadership culture as well as a guide to understanding, empowerment, and how to achieve needed change. I explore this further in Volume 3.

Silence and Abuse. The thread of abusive behavior runs throughout this book series because it is so prevalent in leadership culture. When it comes to silence and abuse the most difficult part of it is the attempts to deny negative women's experiences with male privilege, toxic relationships both male and female, bullying, gaslighting and objectification which are crazy-making. These attempts cause the woman to second-guess or question her experiences while knowing that they were very real.

Resorting to silence is easier until articulation is possible because life in a colluding society is more vicious than kind and more vitriolic than sympathetic when the woman does find courage to break her silence – even if they break the silence in numbers. The social problem of domestic violence and abuse of women is one that shows up in myriad places. The workplace is not excepted from the encroachment of violence against women in the form of abusive leadership culture.[17] Such a workplace environment leaves behind the lingering feelings of being unsafe, of suppressed anger, persistent fear, gnawing anxiety, accusatory guilt and shame which are hallmarks or silent witnesses of this phenomenon. These feelings are the overt evidence of powerlessness in a world where 'patriarchal power' rules. Silence is a powerful and insidious partner of emotional abuse when we look at it through the lens of the Duluth Model of Power and Control[18] in domestic violence -except it is perpetrated outside of the home in the workplace and in society. The issue is about controlling access to power, controlling the cultural narratives, and economical, physical and psychological aspects of women's lives. The personal consequences to women can be being forced to sign non-disclosure agreements, isolation from destroyed work and personal relationships, their support systems such as co-workers, friends and family because they are afraid to talk. Stress, fear, anxiety, being suicidal, having their reputation destroyed and career options taken away. I describe these in Volume 1. So silencing of victims creates a plethora of negative results for the woman. For some women the controlling behavior occurs in the private sphere and they go to work to experience it in the public sphere. Other women do not experience this in the private sphere but experience it in the public sphere or at the workplace. In the process, the realms of threat and danger in women's lives are expanded. The exercise of power and control makes the life and workspaces unsafe and makes the woman hypervigilant.

Outcomes of the Code of Silence

The words that commonly come to mind when the term 'code of silence' is used are no sound, invisibility, no voice, no opinion, absent, no value, disrespect, no consideration, marginalized. how ideological systems and societal structures hinder or impede the fullest development of humankind's collective potential to be self- reflective and self-determining historical actors. Silencing creates invisibility. The maxim that best describes the silence and invisibility is 'out of sight out of mind.' However, invisibility or the silencing of individuals also can occur when they are present. Here's what I mean. Ralph Ellison, author of the *Invisible Man*[19] aptly and powerfully captures this painful reality this way:

I am an invisible man…I am a man of substance, of flesh and bone, fiber and liquids-and I might even be said to possess a mind. I am invisible, understand, simply because people refuse to see me…When they approach me they see only my surroundings, themselves, or figments of their imagination-indeed, everything and anything except me...That invisibility to which I refer occurs because of a peculiar disposition of the eyes of those with whom I come in contact.[19]

Ellison was speaking of the experiences of Black people when he also points out the conflictual aspects of invisibility. Yet segments of the population are invisible because they have been marginalized or excluded from the privileges and opportunities available in society. Their voices, concerns, and needs are silenced, by the dominant society that seeks to secure its majority status and privilege through perpetuating practices and policies that ensure it.[19] For example, the voices of women are also not always heard when they speak. In public, or at meetings. Though what they say can be repeated afterward as someone else's great idea.

Women's concerns are sometimes simply dismissed or disregarded as not important enough to change behavior or practice. These responses are other ways the culture and workplace silences or communicates the invisibility and marginalization of the person. Ellison also argues that there are advantages to being invisible. So, some aspirant women or leaders operate best by flying under the radar – silent and undetected. But Ellison also clearly describes the tiresome and frustrating nature of invisibility as something that is "rather wearing on the nerves," that results in "constantly being bumped by those with poor vision" since they don't really *see* you, or as a convenient contrivance that leaves one to question or "often doubt if you really exist."[19] There have been instances where I have been ignored, bypassed to address the person behind me as if I did not exist. Johnson succinctly describes this as a "metaphor for social alienation" or "the blinding social illusions that render races and individuals invisible to each other."[20]

Women facing these persisting barriers can become isolated and marginalized, though they may be operating in a position that is central to the company as an employee and as a manager; sometimes even as CEO. This isolation and marginalization can be very detrimental to the women's ability to thrive or advance their careers and lives. Here's why. When people are under-represented, excluded and marginalized that positioning embodies a feeling of alienation and frustration in attempts to relate and assimilate to the dominant culture. Exclusion from full participation fosters the perception of being subject to consensus judgment made and enforced by men upon whom women have been historically socialized to be dependent on or to look for protection. In the workplace women can be excluded from key information networks, or as leaders the work evaluations will show negative especially with male subordinates when consensus judgment is made with gender bias.

These women are silenced because they may be alone in the company or department, and believe their experience is theirs alone. The connection of the societal dots have not been made because they are silent about their experiences and more than likely have not articulated them to others in their lives or circles that could help them situate their experience in the broader sociocultural context.

Leadership Implications and Breaking the Code of Silence

The code of silence is ingrained from childhood. The code of silence is a pervasive life-shaping experience for many, supported by society at large. It runs deeper than was originally anticipated. There is the silence of privilege and collusion, the silence of complicity, and the silence of fear, and the silence of marginalization. The voices that are silenced are not at the decision-making table, their needs are ignored or dismissed or quashed. Women also participate in not selecting, or actively hindering other women from access to leadership positions, even though they are fully qualified. All is not well in the sisterhood. This is particularly true in a leadership context where the gender bias, socialization, misogyny, power differentials, and discriminatory cultural influences on decision-making in a patriarchal society. Women's mindsets are also shaped by cultural socialization just like everyone else, and women experience more pressure to conform to expectations for the system to work smoothly. I have observed and heard other women say they are not going to select, vote for, or support a woman's leadership because of tradition. There is also the Queen Bee phenomenon, and articles have been written that support and rationalize not voting for helping or selecting a woman just because she is a woman.[21,22] A classic and quite consequential example here that the most vocal adversary to the Equal Rights Amendment was a woman, Phyllis Schafly, who fought tirelessly to ensure that women did *not* get their equal rights guaranteed in the Constitution as an amendment.[23] I describe this in the epilogue of Volume 1. It is almost 100 years since the ERA was first proposed and still one more state is needed to ratify it. Resistance to women's leadership is especially true when it is the first time such a choice is being presented. In the upcoming case study and the narratives spread about women's leadership ability continue to result in a tendency to consider men as leaders and not women. There is no talk about tradition or never having done this before about men who aspire or want to lead. Men are overrepresented in leadership and we don't question the overrepresentation of their gender when it comes to leadership. Why do women not have that same privilege or benefit of the doubt as their male counterparts? The evidence is clear that women are consistently underrepresented so their selection and placement 'should' be a priority. Women also have a positive effect on profitability, the bottom line, complex decision-making and competitive positioning. Yet, we still relatively silent on the problem making a strong business case for women's leadership in a capitalist country.[24] This is a strong signal that the problem goes much deeper than capability, company viability or even the bottom line. What will it take to break the code of silence?

Breaking the Code of Silence

Richards, and others point out: "If we want to bring an end to the silence that divides us and hides our differences, then we need to treat (everyone)… as though they belong.[25] This is inclusion. Denzin and Lincoln also agree that when those voices are finally heard and written, "voices that were previously silenced can speak as agents of social change and personal destiny."[26] This is the main purpose and goal of this book. It is my desire to be an agent of social change in leadership practice and society as a whole and this book is one way of breaking the code of silence with the following goals.

First, I hope that raising awareness of the code of silence will make a difference in the collective consciousness of the home, society, education and the workplace as together they are the locus of transmission of cultural values. Second, it is to expose and address the code's ramifications so women will not remain isolated in their workplace or life experiences caught in the silence trap. Instead, women will take their place as central and empowered as they recognize that other women have had similar experiences. People in society will correctly identify and expose silencing as a cultural problem. Third, the purpose of breaking the code of silence is to open our collective eyes to acknowledge what is happening in plain sight. The myopia created by societal, gender, economic and racial bias causes failure or inability to see or name the effect of silencing and hold perpetrators accountable. Coming out of silence helps to break the code, lessens control of perpetrators, frees the woman and reduces personal guilt or shame. Breaking the silence will facilitate women's regaining personal power.

A NorthStar or plumb line standard for leadership needs to be reset so that the malevolent silence that exists behind the seemingly benevolent theories and practice of contemporary leadership is broken, is a tall order, but is one that needs to be initiated. There is a need to open safe communication spaces so that organizations, sectors and nations can create an atmosphere where women's leadership can thrive and be sustained for the next generation. Communication spaces for example can be formally or informally facilitated, with a purpose to allow leaders and workers to openly discuss the biases and barriers created by the code of silence, and how to change it. This is further detailed in Chapter 16 on learning that results in dialogue and conscientization that results in change. It starts with leaders and executives who are willing to proactively construct a bias-free organization culture. The leader would need to raise awareness, assess standard organization practice and examine areas where bias is identified, then initiate change in the discriminatory policies and practices.

Training executives and leadership teams can identify and report the key places where silencing has a destructive effect and rewarding managers for proactive responses that fix the problem. Leadership teams will need to be intentional about what they say about women's leadership capability or calling out what is said about women because hidden behind the silence is the pervasive perception that women are not effective leaders. By far the most important reason for breaking the code of silence is takes the metaphorical silencer off the gun, so women, male colleagues and leaders can all pinpoint the source of problems. It also eliminates the tendency for leaders to suffer from the Ostrich Syndrome[27] and gives leaders the courage to face, stop being silent about, and deal with the bias. This means policy, behavior and practice must also be changed if women's workplace and leadership experiences are to reflect the quality of skills and competencies women bring to the table. Such recognition will encourage equity and accountability to break the culture of silence empowering women and men to embrace and honor the hard-wire of leadership wherever it appears. A collaborative approach to create a culture where everyone can thrive can then become a company priority. Leaders are called and invited to exercise conscious leadership not just leadership as usual. The next chapter focuses on women's leadership capability, contributions and company benefits of women as leaders.

Précis

The purpose and use of gun-silencers is used as a provocative analogy to describe the silence around persistent under-representation of women in top leadership positions. In this code, silence is personified explored as a powerful broker in the interaction space of privileged and marginalized groups and facilitating socio-cultural and accepted workplace practices. Operating to ensure the success of both sides, as protector and perpetuator, its partners, currency, assets, are identified in the deeply embedded threads in the fabric and culture of work and society. Consequences of silence as a cover for contemporary leadership practice are denial or acting as if it does not exist, failure of leadership responsibility to ensure accountability for the underrepresentation or discriminatory practices within the organization and to act on what will be needed to change the culture into one that fosters women's ability to thrive as leaders.

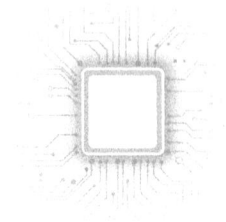

CHAPTER 10

Can Women Lead? The Truth of Women's Leadership Effectiveness

It's not about supplication, it's about power. It's not about asking, it's about demanding. It's not about convincing those who are currently in power, it's about changing the very face of power itself. _ Kimberle Williams Crenshaw

Leadership is about power. But power has historically been the domain of men. Women want to lead, but there is strong resistance to their access to power. But, can women lead? Can women handle power and still be effective? Some would answer yes to these questions; others would respond with an emphatic no. Still others would be ambivalent and middle of the road, unsure or using some sort of exception or qualifier for why more women are not in the top positions or the C-Suite of companies. My response to the questions is yes women can lead, handle power and still be effective. But you really don't have to take my word for it. At an early age girls and young women who are hard-wired to lead don't always exhibit the gendered roles they are socialized to show or act in the ways that are expected. They want to run things, speak up, have a strong opinion, question and sometimes challenge authority that seeks to curtail their freedoms. Leadership skills are evidenced early on that often results in their being called 'bossy' and as they get older being cautioned by their parents to tone down their leadership characteristics and independence if they want to 'find' a husband or be 'liked' by their peers. This is the pressure to conform to expectations. So, there is contradictory information and specific behaviors being encouraged which may be at odds with the woman's hard-wire to lead. These conflicting mindsets remain in play as counter-voices beneath the research findings on preparation, effectiveness and outcomes of women's leadership that I will present. The voices are always there. The internal volume decreases when she operates according to her hard-wire

In this chapter, I address the disconnect between the evidence of women's ability to lead and their representation in top leadership positions. I look to clarify and answer the question what do we know about women's effectiveness when in power? I hope that looking at this question will help to clarify what can happen when a woman's hard-wire to lead is aligned with leadership opportunity. There's a chance to examine the effectiveness of women's leadership and look at the challenges she faces in top leadership positions. With an eye toward proposing company culture system changes that have potential to shape leadership practice into one that is more favorable and open to the contributions women bring to the table. If leadership is a neutral position, then the possibilities for women should be endless. However, as we will soon see this is not always the case.

Forms of Leadership Preparation

The development of leadership skills and preparation for leadership comes from various places. Sports is considered a place where leadership is developed. For instance, Leaders carry a financial or personal risk based on the performance of the organization. The risk associated with winning in the game is termed as having 'skin in the game' or having a stake in the outcome of the engagement whether good or bad and is linked to accountability for winning. I am an avid football fan. The analogy of football is often raised as a descriptor for American culture, business and leadership practice and individual behaviors.[1] It is a male dominated sport in which leadership skills are believed to be developed. Players develop skills in strategic planning, teamwork, and decision-making.

There is a universal perception that people who play or have played sports in their lives are 'automatic' leaders. There is no doubt that knowledge and background help competitors to overcome the opposing team and become winners. As with companies, while all players would love to be on the winning team, there are a limited number of positions or opportunities for those who can play. This confirms one paradigm of leadership: it is conflated with winning. The team that wins is believed to have the better leader. Here's the rub: only a very few men make it to the pro or national level though it may have been a lifelong dream for many. Even there, only one team wins the Super Bowl regardless of the strategy, practices, personal discipline and teamwork. Does this mean that the other teams have failed in leadership? It appears that way because coaches are fired regularly and predictably if they cannot produce a winning team. Does it mean that players who don't make it to the pro level cannot lead? Not necessarily. Football is a game and a business, with an intriguing mixture of physicality, skirting the edge of overt violence, danger and competitive strategy. Football is also surrounded by much glamour, hype, high stakes and billions of dollars. Since leadership is in the arena of real life, the leadership skills learned must be transferable to the workplace. This transfer of perceived leadership skills and competencies are very readily accepted (even sought after) in the workplace or community when the players retire and become entrepreneurs after just a few years. Leadership practice also takes lessons from sports in terms of mindset, discipline, strategy, teamwork and winning. This can be considered as one form of leadership preparation.

Another form of leadership preparation in contrast is the skills women develop as they manage the home and the family responsibilities. It is difficult to fathom why the leadership responsibilities of motherhood -which is not a game- are also not considered to be foundational to developing important leadership skills. Dee Dee Myers states "I am endlessly fascinated that playing football is considered a training ground for leadership, but raising children isn't."[2] This cultural perspective on how leadership skills are developed gender biased and frustrating because it is one-sided, and privileges or elevates the experiences of men and ignores the salient more directly related experiences of women. I take a similar perspective to Myers as the leadership skills of mothers are described in Chapter 8. It might be prudent for leadership practice to take lessons from the leadership skills developed in the home place.

As indicated in the list of leadership skills outlined in Chapter 8, the responsibility to develop children from the early years to adulthood is a billion dollar industry, requires discipline and sacrifice. Raising children is not glamorous, and there is not much hype except in the family of the new addition. The management, leadership, teamwork, coaching, covert or overt strategy, and legacy building skills are honed daily and become increasingly complex as the children get older. Unlike football the mother's work is year-round, not seasonal in terms of engaging the game. The pay is non-existent. The job is physically demanding, and the context may include life threatening violence. But the stakes are exceptionally high. Her skin in the game? The viability of the next generation and communities, countries, nations and culture. How the family 'turns out.' Sometimes the woman wins, sometimes she loses, either way she is responsible. Motherhood generally does not have an early retirement after a couple of years, instead many have to work outside the home, or take on work later; they cannot really be 'fired,' from this job. They remain mothers for life, though women have been let go because of negligence or incapacity and adoption.

There is clearly a disconnect and a false narrative built around the leadership capacity of women and that of men. Some men tend to shy away from, dismiss, or consider these unrelenting responsibilities as menial, or unimportant, as they lead in companies as CEO's where the same skills are needed. Other men fully engage and are involved. The disconnect is evident in the prevailing perception that women cannot lead (with some exceptions), that women do not deserve to be paid equally for the same work, and that they do not deserve equal consideration for promotion and access to leadership opportunity. Instead, in the contemporary leadership context women continue to be punished in myriad consequential ways for pregnancy and maternity leave, with sexual and economic violence. Yes. This attitude has been ever so slowly changing in our society. However, the perceptual and practice changes are certainly not keeping up with women's presence and readiness to lead in the workplace. The perceived ability to transfer these leadership skills and competencies are not readily accepted (or sought after) in the workplace. In fact, the evidence suggests that women are demoted or re-entered in positions lower than the ones they held when they left. They are not usually brought into the organization with a leadership position in mind, instead they are relegated to what is termed the "mommy tracks"[3]. with all its limitations and barriers to self-determination and career advancement.

Either way, preparation for leadership is necessary, and women have taken it seriously. Women are educationally, experientially, and professionally prepared to lead. Here's the evidence: Education statistics indicate quite a clear picture, for example, showing that women have led in the area of degree completion for at least a decade.[3] Perry reluctantly confirmed that women out-earned their male counterparts in degrees at all levels; and that "2009 marked the year when men officially became the "second sex" in higher education by earning a minority of college degrees at all college levels from Associate's degrees up to Doctoral degrees."[4] Perry however, asks the question from a reverse-discrimination perspective of gender- discrimination, "what do they propose be done about female over-representation in higher education at every level and in 7 out of 11 graduate fields?"[5] My response is why not place them in top leadership positions then? If women are better prepared, why would organizations want those who are less prepared to be their leaders? It is this disconnect and non-congruence that has peaked my attention.

Even today, getting an education is still touted as one of the reasons women are not promoted. If this data is accurate, there is evidence that contradicts this education requirement on its face. It also means that their male counterparts are receiving promotions and top positions without the education requirement being fulfilled. So, there is a gender-based leadership gap.[6] The leadership gap can be seen across fortune 500 companies, finance, legal, on boards, in healthcare, medicine, education, technology, advertising, and government. Women were told to close the gap they needed educational credentials. Women have outperformed their male colleagues in gaining education credentials. Yet, the gender-based leadership gap persists, and a clever new narrative is being developed. The rationale is not designed to respond to the unchanged leadership gap. Rather the storyline seeks to craft a reverse discrimination argument against women's higher education. For instance, Schow picks up a similar and convenient argument framing it as an earnings choice vs. gender wage gap.[7] Schow claims that women's choices for their careers are what results in earning less pay. In the process he conflates the leadership gap with the wage gap problem and women not being 'in demand' or not seeking higher paying positions. Both gaps are the result of gender bias, but I disagree that it is because of choice alone. Women's choices are based on the options they must choose from and the level of difficulty to access certain fields. Women continue to be blocked from access into careers that are male dominated. They are also blocked from top leadership positions even in female dominated careers. This creates economic double jeopardy based on gender bias. Thus, the problem is not about career choices but is a result of biased policies, unfair leadership culture and discriminatory practice in relation to promotion and compensation.

Now the wage gap is very real, pervasive and longstanding. Wage inequality is present in both female and male dominated careers and operates even though women have been educationally and formally prepared. Silence plays a huge role as many companies rely on it to sustain and perpetuate inequality. The wage gap has four drivers: 1) unequal pay for women in the same jobs as their male counterparts across all industries, 2) pay inflation for men as opposed to women in male dominated careers. This gender-based value for work shifts depending on which profession men seek or have begun to dominate. Examples include Secretarial positions formerly dominated by men, now are filled mostly by women. Technological positions once also filled by women are now mostly filled by men to the exclusion of women. In both industries the salary ranges and worker value have shifted downward for secretaries and upward for technology, 3) systemically deflated earnings in female dominated jobs, and for women across all sectors, and 4) perceptual devaluation of women's work that results in their persistently being underpaid. Paradoxically, this imbalance continues to manifest for men in female dominated jobs, who still also tend to earn more or hold more top positions than their female counterparts while women remain underpaid in male dominated professions. But as we will soon see the problem is not even this simple. It isn't only about gender bias it is about achieving access, equity, and economic parity regardless of field and discipline of choice.

In Volume 1 Chapter 5 *She Works Hard for the Money* I address economic abuse and violence in detail.[8] The connection here is between acknowledging the value and worth of women and compensating them for the effectiveness of their productivity and leadership, as if they matter.[9] Equally. The wage disparity is not unique to the United States but is especially perplexing in a country that prides itself on liberty and justice for all and on being a global advocate for human rights. Along this same vein, here are other related questions. Why is it the United States, a country that considers itself to be the leader of the free world is still struggling to hire a consummately competent and qualified woman to lead it after 240 years of existence? What does it say about the maturity of the country and its leadership culture when other countries, including developing countries, have already successfully taken that step? If not now, when? With these questions in mind let's look at the truth of women's leadership effectiveness.

The Truth About Women's Leadership Effectiveness

In Fortune 500 companies, the top of the leadership ladder is precarious, lean, and scarce for women. Scholars agree that a range of obstacles exist: informal organization barriers, lack of access to relevant social networks, perceptions of women.[10] Yet, to tell the truth, women such as Joyce Banda, Gen. Lori Berman, Bhenazir Bhutto, Ursula Burns, Elizabeth Dole, Andrea Jung, Golda Meir, Angela Merkel, Ava Peron, Suzanne Shank, Margaret Thatcher, Meg Whitman are on a time-tested list of women who have led successfully across corporate sectors, in national and international settings. They have clearly made their mark in the leadership arena as powerful examples of strong proven leadership some in male dominated industries. The results of their leadership effectiveness present a powerful picture of whether women can truly lead.

Yet, women's representation in top leadership positions remains a notable challenge. Women make up more than 50% of the workforce, and 40% of the managerial staff. Yet, only four percent (4%) of women hold top leadership positions in fortune 500 companies. Just 12 % hold leadership positions in public office; though more than 58% of them have earned college degrees and hold a 51% of middle-management positions.[9,11] These statistics present a troubling picture that pushes at the central focus of this work. The conversation surrounding the workplace context or environment, or what I call leadership culture that sustains this counter-productive phenomenon. If you have ever asked yourself why there are so few women leaders in top executive positions? Why women are persistently undervalued and underpaid at 76% or less on the dollar than their male counterparts?[12] Or, why, if they hold a leadership position, they are often treated with disrespect, underpaid, their competence dismissed as irrelevant, or their leadership neutralized? Are there benefits to women's leadership?

There are noticeable benefits that accrue within organizations with women in top executive and leadership positions. Evidence suggests that corporations with women leaders do better competitively, show greater increases in revenue, and have a more inclusive organization culture. Data consistently shows that when women lead companies or serve on the board, it has a strong positive effect at the corporate and at the macro-economic levels.[12] Anderson conducted a recent comprehensive study of 21,980 publicly traded companies in 91 countries, identified what is now called "Estrogen effect." This 'new' phenomenon reveals that "having at least 30% of women in leadership positions, or the "C-suite," adds 6% to net profit margin."[13] Noland and Moran also confirm that "more women in the C-Suite translated into higher profits."[14] Somehow this data indicates a deeper problem and issue at work if this knowledge and capacity for revenue generation is available to a capitalistic society, and they don't take advantage of this quite prevalent opportunity for revenue generation. To add scope and context to this paradox, or to examine what evidence has been found on women's leadership effectiveness I will begin a brief review of the research.

Ultimately, leaders are judged by their perceived effectiveness in achieving the organization vision and goals. Eagly and Johnson's meta-analysis points out that when we speak of leadership effectiveness it is good to keep in mind that success is "contingent on features of the group or organizational environment.' Further, their analysis found that "women's leadership styles were more democratic than men's even in organization settings."[15] Dubrin's research with over 1800 male and female managers identified some differences between men and women's leadership skill tendencies: women were "rated higher on relationship-oriented leadership skills" while men were "... rated higher on task-oriented leadership skills." However, the general findings indicated that on "overall [leadership] effectiveness, the sexes were perceived the same."[16] Hoyt's research confirms that although women are less likely to negotiate or promote themselves for leadership positions, "women are no less effective at leadership, committed to their jobs, or motivated for leadership roles than men."[17] And, I would add, their contributions are well worth equal pay for equal work. It is important to establish women's leadership effectiveness and ability at the outset because it sets up an important premise for examining the challenges, tensions, and inconsistencies that will be highlighted in the upcoming chapters. As a population group that contributes at least 1% of global wealth; and to 50% of the workforce women are and will continue to be a force to be reckoned with.[17] However, there are conditions that affect perceptions of their leadership effectiveness.

It is general knowledge and visible in organizational practice that women are the lynch pins of most organizations as middle managers, administrative and executive assistants, and secretaries. In their mostly supportive leading roles that make the company run smoothly, they are crucial to company survival, just as it is known that their leadership role is vital for the survival of the family. These two are linked because it appears here that the position and perception of women's role and capabilities have been transposed to the workplace. The perception of the importance of women's leadership ability, though obvious, has been transferred with negative identification to their leadership roles in the workplace -positionally, and economically.

Paustian-Underdahl and their colleagues[18] found the following conditions are contextual factors with potentially positive moderating impact on the perceptions of women's leadership effectiveness. The study examined the moderating factors of time, leadership styles, gender role expectations, prejudice, the double standard, organizational hierarchy (skill requirements at different levels in the company), self vs. other ratings, tokenism, self-esteem and context, and representation (sheer numbers) and their potential effect on perceptions of women's leadership effectiveness. They are presented here to raise awareness of contextual factors, some of which will be addressed in further detail in the upcoming chapters.

- *Time.* Just the passage of time has shown an increasing number of women in the workplace, normalizing their presence and displaying their competence; helps to lessen the incongruity between women and leadership, and the stereotypical association of men with leadership.

- *Leadership styles.* In an increasingly dynamic and fast-paced global leadership context it is proposed that a more feminine leadership style would be needed. These include more communicative, and participative characteristics for effectiveness.

- *Role expectations.* These are still gendered role expectations based on sex-based division of labor. Women encounter more disapproval when operating in positions violating these role-based prescriptive behaviors -such as in leadership positions.

- *Prejudice.* Women leaders face prejudice based on incongruence between characteristics of women and the requirements of leadership roles. This prejudice persists despite evidence to the contrary.

- *The Double Standard.* Barriers to achieving leadership positions can result from the double-standard. But a presence in high status agentic top positions communicates exceptional competence.

- *Organizational Hierarchy* (skill requirements at different levels in the company). Lower level skills are perceived to be gender neutral. Either men or women can fulfill them. Middle level skills are more relational and developmental, so better suited to women. Upper level skills considered to be agentic with higher status, thus more suited to men.

- *Self vs. Other Ratings.* The more male subordinates, the more important the stereotypical qualities and the stronger the lack-of-fit perception of women become.

- *Tokenism.* Women or minorities in this position face exaggerations of difference, higher visibility, greater scrutiny from the majority group; they are excluded from informal activities.

- *Self-esteem and context.* Women tend to underrate themselves due to low self-esteem, attributing success to external factors. Men on the other hand tend to rate themselves higher due to higher self-esteem and self-confidence.

- *Representation* (sheer numbers). The more women in leadership positions the greater their perceived effectiveness. So, recognition of effectiveness comes with aggregate mass of proof that no longer can be ignored or denied. This is juxtaposed with resistance to increasing the numbers of women to the point it makes a difference.

A considerable amount of factors to consider. Highlighting the conditions of perceived effectiveness of women's leadership is critical at this point because the focus of the book goes far beyond just leader competencies to address areas that are usually subsumed within a competency paradigm. The discussion on social role theory addresses this in part; the specific barriers that precede this section will identify several non-competency related concerns that have significant impact on women's leadership opportunities. Even if women were to simply act on their hard-wire to lead, exercising the will to lead and honoring their hard-wire to lead, occurs in the face of underrepresentation, prejudice, challenges to their authority, second guessing, insubordination, ongoing vulnerability, unnaturally high or double-standard of conflicting expectations, and those who would 'force' them in line with the status quo they are destined to change[19] This very difficult leadership culture would most certainly have an effect on the access to leadership opportunity, and expected leadership styles of women because they have to develop and draw on an entirely different repertoire of styles and competencies than men do to lead their followers effectively. Here's what I mean.

There are two general views of the differences in leadership styles based on gender. First that there are no real differences in expression and use of leadership styles based on gender. Second that there are real differences or approaches to leadership and that those differences favor women's leadership styles.[20] When it came to more specific styles, women were generally not found to select relationship oriented over task-oriented styles; rather the gendered social role influences on the context in which they worked dictated which styles were more prevalent. Nonetheless, consistently, women were found to exceed men in the use of democratic, participatory and transformational leadership and styles "that are associated with contemporary notions of effective leadership."[20,21] Recall from earlier, that the kind of group and the organization culture the leader operated in, determined the leaders perceived effectiveness. Contemporary leadership for women has unique challenges with both factors. The leadership effectiveness I have looked at has mainly related to the context and culture. While women's leadership will inevitably change leadership culture and practice, the kind of follower still makes the difference in terms of effectiveness. Followers are becoming increasingly engaged in the leadership process and the desired outcomes.

Followers are seeking to collaborate and participate in the leadership experience. This has become more and more evident: creative follower involvement range from protests, the truth-telling Town Halls, the Valentine's cards, delivery of baked goods, persistent marches and signs with their unique opinion on the issues, followers no longer remain silent. Followers' organic movement is to have their say in how leadership is carried out. Influencing leadership is the beginning of a revolution of awareness in the people. Followers are beginning to realize that the exercise of their power, voice and visibility is amplified more as a collective group than as individuals because they are indeed 'stronger together'. The voices of followers are now recognizing their collective power to hold leaders accountable for their actions.

Leaders do have power and influence over their followers. An apt description of the leader's power was provided for us in Palmer's book *Leading from within: Reflections on spirituality and leadership*. In it he states: "A leader is a person who has an unusual degree of power to create the conditions under which other people must live and move and have their being—conditions that can either be as illuminating as heaven or as shadowing as Hell."[22] In my years of work experience, employees spend 8-16 hours working. Imagine if those hours are spent in a toxic work environment. Yet, leadership culture is where the 'alpha male' syndrome shows up and can play a significant role in perceptions of women's leadership effectiveness. Alpha males can embody both the Heaven and the Hell characteristics. I have written about the abusive leadership context and culture and the abusive demoralizing behavior is directly related to the negative side of alpha male leaders or co-worker characteristics. The positive characteristics according to Ludeman and Erlandson[23] of commanding, visionary, strategist and executors are all essential leadership behaviors. However, the need of the alpha male to control their surroundings and the followers involved can end up creating an authoritative leadership culture which fosters a context rife with domineering, intimidating, abusive, micromanaging and controlling behaviors that can be quite demoralizing and destructive to company viability. The potential for these behaviors to occur is quite high given the overrepresentation of males in leadership practice. It also sets up a follower environment where controlling behavior can become threatening, overbearing and abusive as has been clearly laid out in the image, sex, economic and ethics codes described in Volume 1. Performance evaluations; absenteeism, perception of insubordination when something cannot not be done "right away" or stress from unethical actions the leader wants, expects, and is willing to reward you to do can all be affected in the abusive and manipulative work environment. The question then becomes what are the implications for leadership under these circumstances?

Implications for Women's Leadership

What does this mean for women's leadership? Women who are hard-wired to lead are usually some of the best and brightest, professionally prepared candidates to grace organizations. They are not risk averse: Professional preparation often includes significant relational, cultural, economic and socio-political risk. If this form of leadership includes serving the followers, developing, valuing and nurturing them, then I would argue that these skills or even characteristics are inherent and deeply ingrained in many women: traits, characteristics or tendencies that are built in to some extent, or developed and refined in other contexts. If the data alone were taken into consideration, women would be poised to become the next wave of the 21st century's global leadership society, as the skills they have are now in demand. Or so one would think or hope. However, we have begun to see that there are deeper challenges in the leadership context that will be examined.

Some argue that we have not made the connection of these dots clearly enough; or that the business case has not been made. Not so. The business case has been made, the statistical evidence is clear as more and more research piles up supporting the net positive, net profitability, affect women at the top levels in companies have because of their innovation, and complex decision-making ability. The persisting under-representation belies a stated operational hypothesis (hiring the best and the brightest for leadership positions) that has become a reality for only a few women if the statistical data is anything to go by. The work of Paustian-Underdahl, Walker and Woehr[24] suggests that when "rated by a majority of female raters, female leaders were seen as more effective than men" and that women were rated significantly more effective than men in business and educational settings, in mid- and upper level positions, because of perceptions of extra competence when they held upper level positions.[20] This indicates that as higher numbers of women are placed at the executive leadership levels, the perceptions of women's leadership effectiveness will become more positive because of the frequency. This in turn increases the possibility of more women being placed in top leadership positions. Some argue that women have increasingly had opportunity to assume leadership roles in an ever-broadening range of disciplines, fields, and organizations. Generally, that is true. However, the paucity of those with opportunity to make it, as well as the protracted pace of their advancement, sustains the intrigue and concern surrounding this phenomenon.

As a result, we can conclude there is robust evidence to support women's leadership effectiveness and benefits to the companies they lead. However, that leadership effectiveness occurs in a culture which is antagonistic in which women's leadership is questioned and challenged even as they continue to rise to the top positions. Women have and are undeniably demonstrating their competency, skill, and effectiveness on world stages. The discussion on why this is so centers primarily on the persistent perception of women's capability and effectiveness in leadership. Most often the perceptions are filtered through the lenses of gendered prejudicial biases against women who would be operating outside of their prescribed societally sanctioned social roles as leaders. Executive and leadership coaching that identifies and pinpoints the alpha male leader as the source of some of the company problems becomes vital with at least three major benefits.

First would be to reduce the negative alpha male qualities[23] that create an abusive leadership culture, destructive manipulative management while preserving the positive qualities. Leaders and women must be vigilant that women who lead are not forced to adopt the negative alpha male behaviors but lead in their own unique way. Second, a strategic breaking of the silence to hold leaders accountable for the impact of abusive behaviors and to develop a plan to change the culture. This inclusive culture would be one where women's effective leadership capability, competence and ability to deliver profit gains translates into hiring or promoting more women into top leadership positions. Third, the placement of more women in leadership positions to balance the leadership styles would improve the context and create a more positive perception of women's leadership.

Obviously, women's relational and democratic leadership characteristics transcend the leadership of just children. Nonetheless the private context most certainly provides the leadership skills that are needed for contemporary followers. This expertise must be integrated as easily into the broader context of leadership as the skills developed on the field or court because relational skills are increasingly needed. The leadership context and culture in which women seek to lead has potential for change to one that is more inclusive to the competencies and capabilities that women embody and bring to the table. In this way inclusion opens up significant potential for changing the perception of women's leadership effectiveness. One final consideration is that women have gone to great lengths to be educationally and experientially prepared to be ready to take advantage of every opportunity presented to them to lead. Followers today are increasingly knowledge workers, subject matter experts, thought leaders, and highly educated professionals. The fact that women also leading in educational and professional preparation sets them up to lead or work with the new type of follower who increasingly wants to participate and collaborate in decision-making and co-constructing a mutually beneficial and strategic future of the organization.

Contextual moderators, which are frequently missing from the leadership context, analysis and conversation (time, group being led, context of leadership, underrepresentation).[24] Other moderators which also contribute to damaging the perception of leadership effectiveness for women are the stories and narratives that persistently contradict women's leadership effectiveness. I believe these narratives have greater influence on the under-representation and the misperception of women's leadership ability than the evidence of women's leadership effectiveness. Why? Because they perpetuate the culture and reinforce biases or the mindsets and attitudes of decision-makers against women. We take this up in the next chapter. It is my contention that the barriers to women's leadership can only be confronted when the 'shades of truth' that perpetuate the status quo and defy the evidence of women's capacity to lead effectively are challenged, brought to light, and countered with truth.

Precís

There is ample historical evidence of a powerful legacy of women's effective leadership that cannot be ignored. Women have successfully and effectively led companies and countries through times of turmoil, challenge, and transformation. Yet the sticking point of under-representation continues to be problematic if less than 5 percent of top leadership positions are held by women. Successful women leaders may use similar leadership styles as men; however, leading women also demonstrate a distinct, more participative, democratic and transformational leadership characteristics. I believe the effective collaborative leadership styles of women are adapted from their relationship-oriented skills-base and become a means for survival in what would otherwise be challenging leadership contexts.

Though the contexts in which women lead determine how their leadership success and effectiveness is perceived and evaluated, the 'estrogen effect' carries undeniable organizational benefits. Benefits such as increased revenue, competitive positioning and inclusive decision making can be catalysts for the greater appreciation of the relational skills women leaders bring to the table. These skills are increasingly required and present a welcome contrast to the increasing incongruence of autocratic abusive leadership demonstrated by their male counterparts particularly when knowledge workers are implicated. Combined, the skills, benefits and effectiveness incentivise the needed shift in leadership culture to one that is less prejudicial and more receptive to women as leaders, and opens the door to increased access to top leadership positions for women.

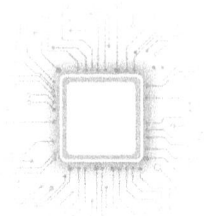

CHAPTER 11

Shades of Truth: Myths, Spins and Double-Standards

"The way to right wrongs is to turn the light of truth on them." _Ida B. Wells

"I swear to tell the truth, the whole truth, nothing but the truth so help me God" is the oath that a witness takes before they sit down to testify. If the witness does not tell the truth or makes a false statement, the witness has committed perjury.[1] Most often perjury occurs to obstruct justice and or to protect someone. Lying under oath is a criminal offense that must meet two general criteria: that an actual lie was told and willful intent to tell it. It is quite unsettling then, to see and hear telling the truth so ubiquitously disregarded in our contemporary discourse, society and in the workplace. People and companies don't always present the truth -even with truth in advertising laws. Lies are color coded to distinguish and categorize them based on the severity of impact on others, or to justify levels of acceptability.[2]

As children, we would be punished for not telling the truth, or if we were caught in a lie. There was a time when a person's word was his or her bond. However, it is difficult to hold someone to their word, or even have a way to bind them to it when it changes daily or even several times a day. Today people can get a 'pass' for not telling the truth. False statements are considered at minimum something which was 'not meant' that the hearer somehow 'misunderstood' what was heard, or that the words were 'nothing to be concerned' about. Even truth descriptors have shifted over time from lie, to misspeak, to alternative facts or an evolution of position just to name a few. In the process, society is slowly lowering truth standards, creating new levels of 'acceptability' of lies based on the situation, and removing horizons of significance of truth claims.[3] As the concept of truth is examined in this chapter, I will highlight the culture and conditions that lend themselves to truth telling or truth construction. Then, to make the connection to women's leadership I provide a description of myths and spins of truth that are utilized as operational frameworks for shaping perceptions of women who want to lead. I also examine how myths, spins, mistruths, and an unfair double-standard shape our perception and understanding of women's leadership experience in the contemporary work environment and leadership context and culture. Perception and reception of truth is always in context which comprises the people involved, the issue at hand, and what people are willing to believe. So, let us look at truth in context.

Over 2000 years ago a man called Pilate asked the question 'What is Truth?[4] In the face of the truth-claim the man before him had presented. The truth-claim was accurate, and Pilate acknowledged it, but did not act on it. He abdicated his responsibility as leader, placing the onus of the decision on the people as part of the decision-making context. This resulted in an innocent man's death by crucifixion. There is a distinction made between the Truth and truths. The former is based on whether it aligned or supported with real facts, events, or things; the latter is relative to context or the narrator.[5]

Truth is what is left standing after all other truth claims have been compared to it and have fallen. From this perspective truth can be checked and verified. The latter truths, on the other hand, are based on someone's construction and the acceptance or belief of that construction to be true by others. These truths are relative, can be alternative representations of truth, false, partially true or perceived to be acceptable in the moment. When checked these accounts may be factually untrue. Truth is also standards-based. The standards are like what Taylor in the book *Ethics of Authenticity* calls horizons of significance.[5] When truth standards are ignored or dismissed an erosion, (a breakdown or alteration) of truth occurs. The standard of reference as a measure or plumb-line by which statements can be checked for accuracy is shifted or diminished in importance as a guide rail. Thus, the Fact-check takes what is said or put forth as truth and comparatively examines it for veracity. What occurred or was said is either confirmed as true or untrue. The issue then becomes what is the public's response when declarations are found not to be true, or to what level the alteration of truth is allowed to be taken. Will the lie be accepted as truth or not? Will truth remain a requirement for credibility? Or will both truth and lie be equally acceptable?

When Shaded Truth Prevails.

Today, there are numerous platforms that allow many voices to provide information. The value of the many technological platforms and social media outlets available to us gives everyone a voice. This is a good thing. However, the sources of information available are overwhelming and some of these sources are considered to be influencers because they have millions of followers. There is a game called Telephone where someone would start a circle of conversation by whispering in the ear of the person next to them. Each person in turn whispers what they heard in the next person's ear. In the game the information was to be passed on to the next person in sequence until everyone had heard, and it had circled around to the person who had shared the original information. The goal was to see how much the information had changed as it made its way around the circle. Players were usually surprised, laughed about and discussed how the phrase had changed, trying to identify where and how that change had occurred. It was a humorous way to illustrate how true information could be distorted or altered as it is passed from one person to another. Fast forward to include our technological platforms with the access to many people and you can begin to imagine how truth can easily be distorted, especially if the intent is to deliberately provide misinformation. In this game the alteration of information occurs innocently and spontaneously.

However, here I address how truth claims and information about women's leadership can be altered and deliberately spread through narratives to preserve systemic practices in culture and in the workplace on what we are to believe and how women are to be treated in relation to their leadership. One thing that is increasingly clear in a way that is unprecedented is that truth is quite frequently constructed by the teller as long as there is a group of individuals with propensity to believe, and act on such constructed truth (or a self-created reality), while dismissing the actual, factual Truth, and questioning its existence.

Sire, in the book the *Universe next door* [6] discusses the concept of worldviews. One of the defining criteria of worldviews is how we view truth and use language. He uses the answers to 7 questions to illustrate how the philosophy of life cultures or communities change across eras and how the resulting worldviews or conceptions of life are redefined or reshaped over time. The greatest shift in worldview, or the way we view the world, between the modern and postmodern worlds has been in relation to how language is used to construct meaning. In the process truth has a stronger relationship to relativism than to fact or standard for some individuals. By that I mean in a post-modern world truth is relative, based on personal preferences and or what it is linguistically constructed to be, and the meaning the construction holds for us.[5,6]

For example, when a narrative is constructed, if it is not factual, it can be deemed credible if the person who created it can get a group to believe and support the claim. It is also essential to appreciate that the constructed stories frequently provide both control and benefit to the storyteller. How does that happen? In Nietzsche's 'Übermensch'[7] the self is held to be above the truth, the self can be the creator of convenient truth and believes truth can be shaded or manipulated for their benefit in the moment. Truth on these terms is considered a disposable commodity, something that is important or useful for interaction with the community that believes and operates by it. Thus, shaded truth can prevail when the storyteller has a reason for presenting that version of reality. In this scenario a person can make up who they are, what their worth is, create a false lifestyle impression, and shape others' perception of them all by the narratives that they promote.

The power of this approach lies in the group or community that believes and buys into the story. This goes beyond comparing a lie or mistruth to verifiable facts. Instead shaded truth relies on a narrative or story that allows the definition and construction a self or identity of a person or community that may have nothing to do with actual reality. The narrative or story is portrayed, and operated on, as if it is reality for the benefit of the storyteller in the moment. This self is constructed by language and words and so, it is what Sire describes in detail as an insubstantial self (intangible and of no substance). In contrast to what creationists believe, that the creator created a substantial self *ex nihilo*, language-created selves remain insubstantial, based on imagination, but can be acted on as if true by those who buy into the fabrication.[6]

One of the significant dangers in engaging in the shades of truth is that, like quicksilver, it changes in form and shape at the whim or perceived need of the individuals who construct it. The changes are ultimately difficult to contain. One way today, another way tomorrow, or several ways in the same day like a chameleon that changes its skin to suit the environment it is in as a means to perfectly blend in or be difficult to see or be detected except by the most discerning eye. I am reminded of children with imaginary friends – invisible but treated as real. Parents and family members will buy into the 'game' and play along with the child, going so far as to leave an empty chair at the table pretending it is the imaginary friend's seat. Sometimes sitting on the imaginary friend if they forget to play along. The imaginary 'friend' takes preeminence in the child's life and can encroach on the lives of the adults around them if they have initially chosen to buy into the fantasy narrative. The imaginary friend is insubstantial. A figment of the child's imagination. Make-believe narratives of insubstantial selves have been assisted by technology and social media. The focus, in passing here, is on the technologically enabled avatars and personas that individuals can use to create or alter what they look like in the online or social media worlds. In this space, the identity presented to others can be quite (and intentionally) different from the real person. Sometimes, that social media persona allows users to show who they really are because it can be anonymous.

The insubstantial persona that has been created and presented can be an alter ego to the person in real life. When it comes to women's leadership, the cultural conditions must be ready and open to acceptance of shaded truth. There must be conditions and circumstances which favor shaded truth. In the societal settings where shades of truth are prevalent there are also supporting conditions and circumstances that predispose individuals, groups or communities to accept the version of truth, story, or metanarrative that is presented. These conditions can be obvious, and sometimes not so obvious, but they constitute a framework for the operating belief systems.

Conditions for Shaded Truth

Power. The power link is made when the story originates and is perpetuated by the power structure. Power differentials play a crucial role in the narrative that's told, how often it is repeated, and the tendency for it to stick. The differentials I am talking about include men over women, manager over employees. The power in the stories lies in the ability to bring together groups and individuals that would otherwise not be connected. Sire points out "…in every culture there is a sufficiently agreed upon story that acts as a metanarrative…these stories, acting as metanarratives, mask a play for power by those in any society who control the details and the propagation of the story."[8] So, those who are in control of the story and how it is shared also hold power, seek to gain it, or are attempting to maintain it. The power and utility of shading truth also lies in how persistently and frequently the story is told. In abusive situations the power and control further lies in whether the victim remains silent, as the silence allows the perpetrator to continue to distort reality with mistruths and create situations that causes the woman to doubt herself and others to doubt her. With the advent of technology, sheer volume will eventually shorten that timeframe required for the story to spread and attain oppressive qualities.

Time. Time requirement is vital: According to Sire "it takes a long time for ideas to sink into culture."[9] For shades of truth to 'take' or embed themselves in the psyche of the company and society takes time and repetition. This is accomplished through articulating, sharing, and socialization of listeners. The goal through sheer repetition, inundation and normalizing the shade of truth is to ensure that it becomes part of the culture and sounds like the truth. This is how new ideas, practices, cultural changes are introduced and infused into the culture. If there is no clear contrasting truth, or if individuals decide to accept shaded truth in place of factual or verified truth claims entire groups of people, cultures and companies can operate as if shaded truth is a reality. The perceptions of women's capacity and capability to lead, the lack of worth attributed to the contributions that they bring to the workplace are unsubstantiated, disproven forms of shaded truth. Yet companies, and cultures routinely operate on these premises.

Adoption. Contemporarily, we have seen that it takes about a few months with a relentlessconvincing storyteller, the willingness of people to believe that story, and a repetitious news cycle to reinforce that story, for people to act on it. What we have also seen that it can take years to build a narrative in the face of truth that contradicts it. Though the narrative will not stand up to a fact check because of the truth, there can be individuals who will continue to believe and promote it even when confronted with the truth that dismisses it. The evidence to the contrary is ignored, or the storyteller may have changed the narrative because it is no longer of benefit to them. The narrative once adopted is difficult to erase, to change back to non-existence or the time before it existed. It continues to cast doubt or suspicions or becomes a stereotype which is hard to shake. For example, when it comes to women and leadership the narrative is that women cannot, or are not supposed to, lead. This narrative has been in place since the establishment of the nation. The adoption of this narrative is borne out by women's persistent underrepresentation in top leadership positions. There is evidence to the contrary and women have proven they can lead, yet, inexplicably they are rarely chosen to lead.

Shades of Truth and Methods of Integration into the Belief System

Certain conditions must be present to prepare or make it easier for a society's groups to adopt an alternative reality. There must be a certain disposition that opens the people up to willingly receive false information. The conditions include but are not limited to 1) being filled with fear, discontent and dissatisfaction with the current reality or situation, or being ignored or dismissed, 2) if the creator of the narrative fabricates the story because they have a proposed or desired agenda 3) the narrative may be created to rationalize intended actions or to re-shape or reframe reality, to cover up discrimination 4) Agents, including the storyteller must be willing to engage in repetition to normalize, desensitize, and make it sound like truth because it is stated so often 5) There must be an audience listening that needs to buy into it to have their insecurities assuaged or to maintain and perpetuate desired privileges and the status quo , and 6) there also has to be a strategic willingness by those who have bought into the narrative or who will benefit from its existence to take action to maintain protective silence. The silence is kept without concern that such miseducation and misspeaking can ultimately be factually challenged by the truth or by experiences to the contrary. Here, in the case of women's leadership, there is a societal audience that has determined that women can only hold certain roles, and leadership is not one of those roles. The agenda is to keep women out, the rationalization is to explain why women are kept out, and to protect those who keep them out. Those who uphold the code of silence in companies for instance are leaders who stand to benefit from not allowing women to access the roles. There is evidence that women can and do lead, but the adoption of the false narrative continues to remain as a barrier for women.

Erosion. When we look at erosion, I am focusing on one vital condition which is the openness to removal of cultural horizons or any standards or boundaries. This is also a descent of society down the slippery slope of cultural change and consensual relaxation (or elimination) of traditional truth boundaries based on fact.[10] Erosion is a collective shift in preference for constructed truths based on the individual's truth and desired community realities that can potentially supersede fact-based truth. The pushing back against societal boundaries can just be acting as if the norms no longer exist. Boundary removal also signals that the new standards that are being set and normalized are much lower than the ones being removed and dismissed – because they are based on personal ethics, agendas, and motivations. Thus, the framing of narratives can take the form of

- The construction of alternative identities that are more glamorous and suitable to the life and identity we imagine as opposed to the reality that we live. It would be important to create and sustain a new narrative closer to the truer perception of women's leadership capability to justify their non-selection to the top leadership positions for example.

- Followers who would rather not (or who do not have the courage or personal fortitude to) accept responsibility for working with the leader to realize the change that is necessary. They would rather accept or buy into a collective story presented by the leader which 'appears' to answer the dilemma of their reality. Because it is insubstantial and fabricated or constructed, the answer to the dilemma of reality will not appear. But, it can take time for 1) disillusionment to set in; 2) recognition that the work to co-create a solution must still be done, 3) taking action to reject the constructed story, and 4)seeking another leader that will co-construct a reality that is closer to truth and one that moves forward toward a mutually created future. In both of these scenarios there is an unrealistic narrative that is found out, but the shame or discomfort in rejecting the false narrative and returning to the truth standard can now be problematic for those who accepted it in the first place. So, let's look at the circumstances that push believers of a false narrative away from the original standard.

Circumstances Ripe for Shades of Truth

There are environmental conditions that make it more favorable for shades of truth to be created and used. Nothing happens in a vacuum. An example would be where a society's context needs the narratives to exist to support undesirable status-quo behaviors. Supporters who agree with and act on the improper behaviors sanctioned by the shaded truth also must tacitly accept the historical precedents that permitted this behavior in the first place. Followers grant conscious or unconscious endorsement of this behavior even though there may be laws against it. There must also be a group(s) of the population that are marginalized, powerless and voiceless and targeted for discrimination. Population groups who are indifferent because they are not personally involved are part of the mix, their mindset is it does not affect me so it does not concern me.

Those who buy into or tolerate the mistruth or are willing to act on it because they like the perpetrator or the new narrative is plausible are the other part of the mix. In these situations, there are silent onlookers and those who believe or give more weight to the half-truth or lie than reality because they believe one person's word over another.

So, when it comes to a victim's word against the perpetrator, the word of the person who has authority usually wins out or is taken over the victims. Situational examples include policemen and blacks; men over women; bosses over employees; white women over black women. This perceived hierarchy in perceptions of truth and honesty can include outright lies and discriminatory behavior. But as we have witnessed it can have devastating and life-threatening effects on victims. For example, there is the nation's history of slavery and dehumanization that sets up a context of normalized brutality, violence and murder without consequence against Black people. It is particularly insidious when the perpetrators are agents of law and order, and the position of authority is used to abuse women with sexual misconduct.[11] This can also be seen in policing where recent videos showed us one kind of evidence and the report and narrative surrounding the event specifically and diametrically opposed to what is seen with the naked eye. The narrative presented then attempts to convince us that what we saw is not real but insubstantial, but the interpretation or 'story' of what we are witnessing is substantial: the goal being to get enough individuals, but especially the prosecutors and jury to accept and exonerate perpetrators' actions and behavior. Teaching people to not become outraged at what we see with our eyes. The system responds by not charging officers based on the claim of self-defense or feeling their life being threatened when the victim is unarmed. It is interesting here as well that the perpetrators are not averse to constructing a reality that feeds into the accepted narrative of the society. In fact, the narrative must partially tap into one or more aspects of social narratives in order to provide a sense of reality. In the broader culture, it goes back to power differentials based on race in the example I gave, and gender and status when it comes to women and their treatment in the leadership context.

The threat of harm is ever-present in these relationships if the narrative or claim is contradicted with truth by whistleblowers, truth-tellers or silence breakers. The key purpose of shading truth or promoting constructed truth is to mischaracterize a situation or group identity and in so doing they ontologically destabilize the listeners and their way of being. As a result, the consequences are making the listener question what they have heard. Believing things which are not aligned with the standard which makes up our central core or belief system, shakes the foundation of our way of being. Carefully crafted mistruths create epistemological[12] confusion or confusion about what we really know. The resulting uncertainty around what we know begins to shake the original framework of factual knowledge that we once relied on. This uncertainty increases if lies are constantly introduced and repeatedly promoted as being true. In environments where truth is constantly altered or constructed, listeners will have several choices. First is to constantly identify what the facts are and rehearse the truth standards. This is what we know as fact-checking. In order for this to work there must be a known truth, a record or set of facts that dispute the statement presented, and ability to locate the record so that everyone is aware of its existence. In the face of constant lies this can be an exhausting but crucial exercise.

Second is to succumb to the repeated mistruths and begin to readily accept the lies as truth. This increases the normalcy of constant confusion, inner destabilization, and believing what was last heard as compared to the stability of what was once known and accepted as truth originally. Though this choice appears initially easier, it also saps the listener's ability to flex their critical thinking muscle which deteriorates into rationalizing our acceptance of the credibility of this alternate truth based on who it came from. Third, to accept a lie is also easier if people are too busy or overwhelmed to seek out truth on their own. Acceptance of alternate truths is also easier if the person does not have an original truth base that signals something is not quite right with what they are hearing. Fourth, if the listener is in denial about the truth, or struggling to accept it as reality, then the mistruth suddenly becomes the easier option of the two to believe. It is easier to believe a lie when it us framed in authenticity. "I will say what no one else will say" sounds authentic, and it can lull those who are seeking 'authenticity' or who want affirmation of their disbelief in what others have to say. When people do not want to change, they will seek out supporting narratives as perceptual defenses which minimize the feared disruption of change that is needed but which the individual doesn't want to make.

Fifth, constant bombardment of shaded truth, mistruths or constantly introducing lies into the conversation creates socio-cultural fatigue and deep nagging anxiety in the public. The narratives work to destabilize the very foundation of a person's way of being and shake the frameworks of factual knowledge based on truth making us unsure of what we know.[12] Truth can be disruptive, but I believe there must be courage to tell it to keep people centered, aligned, to reduce confusion, anxiety, fear and mistrust. Destabilization of our fundamental way of being and the normative horizons we have had to structure our lives and culture creates anxiety. The anxiety comes from being unsure of what to believe, the fear and fatigue of having to fight off, discern, fact check, or not knowing what to believe or what the end outcome will be.

For example, technology has been a disruptor of the workforce since its inception. Friedman, the author of *The World is Flat* points out that technology fundamentally and permanently changed manufacturing processes, altered procedures, automated how work is done. In the process workers are increasingly displaced by artificial intelligence and robotics even as it has required the need for analysts and created the knowledge worker of today.[13]

Companies and workers were busy integrating technology into the systems but were not adequately preparing themselves for being displaced from work. The truth? New skills and knowledge were going to be required and workers who did not acquire them were displaced by technology or the new skills and knowledge needed for a global green economy. When workers were told that some jobs were not coming back, those who already knew their jobs were threatened shifted from the anxiety of this reality, to denial and anger. The result? Many who wanted affirmation of their disbelief of the truth were lulled into believing that their jobs were coming back because the misinformation matched the need to believe the lies because they were presented as being authentic. Anxiety and anger over being forced to make changes that were needed caused workers to believe a mistruth that neatly fit into the mindset that would not require them to make changes they did not want to make.

The candidate who made the statement that change would be needed was vilified as wanting to take the jobs away. Despite the fact that technology was already noticeably encroaching on or had removed their positions for years, workers chose to believe the other candidate who promised to bring the jobs back. Knowing full well that technology could not be rolled back. Reality? The jobs are not back. The old familiar jobs will more than likely never be back, but new jobs will emerge. It has been fascinating to observe that new candidates are again reiterating the truth that was rejected just a couple years ago. They are presenting the new job reality as new ideas, but the core truth remains the same. Perhaps people are now ready to believe the truth and make the necessary changes or develop the new skills needed for survival. In the socio-cultural context, those who have access to truth and the ability to disseminate it such as media, have a responsibility, as truth police, to be the checks and balances by presenting truth to expose untruths as relentlessly and constantly as the untruths appear. This in itself can be exhausting. I also believe that there should be less excited discussion of the misrepresentations and more reinforcement of the truth that is being eroded. In the workplace context, when we are relating false narratives and alternate truths to women's leadership aspirations there are similar challenges.

Shaded Truth and Women's leadership

The leadership myths and spins function much like a virus does in computer software. It attaches to the hard-wire of the individual and sticks around infecting each experience, interaction, negotiation and performance opportunity that presents itself to the core functionality of the candidate. If not eradicated the virus can scramble and eventually alter the hard-wire into something that is totally unlike what it was intended to be. Some of the 'shades of truth' about women's leadership capacity, have influenced the perceptions, behavior and actions of individuals in leadership culture: the under-representation numbers confirm that. However, as numbers can also potentially indicate that there are less women who make it through. In the workplace, homeplace, and in the church place, where men still currently control the story or metanarrative and the leadership positions, they also control the perception of women's leadership capability.

The narratives around women's leadership were built over time, in a patriarchal societal context and leadership culture while women were absent from the decision-making table in the workplace to show or voice any contrasting view or reality. Though the narrative has shifted somewhat over time by the women who have successfully and effectively led organizations, communities, and nations, the shapers of the narrative have been quite adept at reframing or reshaping the story to counter any advances women have made. There is always something wrong, or there's a problem with what they do right. Weakness, untrustworthiness, lack of professional preparation are all ruses made up as part of the metanarrative to keep top leadership positions just out of the reach of women. It also perpetuates the behavior that result in consequential gender-biased contextual barriers for women.

Consequence of Biased Behavior. As indicated earlier in the chapter, a lie can function as truth if it is accepted and acted on. Taking someone's work and passing it off as yours is not acceptable but is a can be common in workplace practice. It is stunning to see how our society no longer feels the need to fact check statements for truth content. Not only has the terminology changed from softening the word lie to 'misspoke' or 'misrepresented' and alternative facts; we have evolved to trying to decide who should have responsibility to verify or challenge the truth of statements made specifically, purposively and confidently as if they were true when in fact they are not.

Consequence of Underrepresentation. Women's scarcity as leaders also in part serves as a framework for understanding the case analysis that follows in the upcoming chapter. The era in which we live is language-based and post-modern. This is the power of the story, the strength and pervasiveness of the spins. When an individual, or a group of people are silent or silenced, the narrative can be developed without their input. Truth can be abandoned for mistruth, and people can be desensitized to or in denial of mistruths, or not even challenging what is stated as would have been done formerly. The media, as public educators, knowledge creators, investigators and information providers with broad platforms should guard the basic elements of trust in information: truth and integrity. Much like truth in lending[14] truth in knowledge should be the standard and deviations disclosed. It can then be transparent, validated and ultimately reliable and verifiable.

As a society we have failed our women miserably when it comes to equality. Interestingly enough as drivers of the discourse, there is the reality that the media creates an expectation that can be unreasonable in the interest of getting to the knowledge first. Yes, I know that is part of the journalist's job. However, as an observer the anomaly of a woman contending for the top leadership position in the world caused hyper-vigilance on the part of the media on things that were insubstantial and not enough on the substantial information that was presented. The alternative is insufficient coverage that marginalizes and silences them. Ultimately this approach became problematic, perpetuating the myth of ineffectiveness, and the claim of not having heard a clear message.

Myths of Women's Effectiveness as Leaders

Hoyt points out that the research supports "social costs and backlash experienced by women when they promote themselves or are competent in positions of authority."[15] Negative reaction and social costs are compounded with higher risk factors for women of color. According to the research literature, actual barriers against women as leaders are in place, and many experience role conflicts and tensions as they take on leadership roles.[16] One of the myths involves devaluation of women.

This is not only linked to perception of performance but to the wage gap. Devaluing the contributions and authority of female leaders by male subordinates in performance evaluations, and in compensation, and the evidence is a persistent wage gap for women doing the same work. Another myth involves misrepresentation of the effectiveness of women's leadership styles. Misrepresenting the leadership effectiveness of women because their transformational leadership style is different becomes a means to force women to lead more like men. Male subordinates also tend to rate the effectiveness of female leaders lower overall.[17] Then there's the issue of double jeopardy or different requirements and standards for women as opposed to men.

Double Jeopardy

There are several factors that can illustrate double jeopardy. Cost. Attitude and perceptions related to Eagly & Johnson point out "being out of role in gender-relevant terms has its costs for [women] leaders…"[18] In Volume 1, the spotlight shone on the price that women pay for desiring to work and aspiring to lead in terms of image, gender, sex, money and religion. Later in this chapter w see how it is linked to spins, we looked at the whole issue of women's education in terms of the perception of their readiness for leadership. Here women's education is placed under double jeopardy. There can be a requirement for a degree as a prerequisite for a promotion, but a degree can also be the reason a woman is considered overqualified for the position. When it comes to education, research confirms that for the last two decades women have out-performed their male counterparts in degree attainment at all levels.[19] The reality is that not having a degree can become a requirement for promotion for women but having a degree does not always translate into the promotion for women. The woman is held back from promotion because she does not have a degree, but she is not granted the promotion when she has earned the degree. The same is not true for her male counterpart whose promotion may not even be contingent on the degree. The bar is higher for women without similar requirement for male colleagues, this is double jeopardy. A note on Black women in the workplace is captioned in Tomlin's point that "higher academic qualifications do not guarantee success among black people in the employment market."[20]   Schultz adds and interesting twist to the mix when he states "to encourage the schooling of women unleashes an internal political process within families as well as among those interest groups in society who stand to gain or lose"[21] indicating that women's education is not an isolated event, but one that has an impact on the family, the workplace and society. Sometimes it has negative impact with people trying to diminish what has been accomplished. Women's response has been to continue pursuing their education in record numbers.

The Spins on Women's Leadership

This section addresses what are called 'spins'. Spins are a shade of truth that is opposite to reality, usually constructed to make sound or seem better than it actually is. A spin is a story constructed to set and retain the context that supports the status quo. As one of the means used to shade the truth, for the purposes of this discussion the spins are directly opposite descriptors of women's capability. It is a tacit recognition of the woman's areas of strength and a tactical move to assert that the opposite is true. Repetition is essential for this to work. And, when it comes to the workplace, the spins surrounding women's leadership have been in operation for years, thus it is well-entrenched; and presents conscious and unconscious barriers for aspiring women.

Spin of Incomplete Preparation.

One common spin is the constant training recommendation for women who are highly qualified professionally with knowledge, skills, and abilities. This spin is used as a tactical reason for delaying the advancement of women and their careers, while negating their experience, potential and qualifications. It is the perpetual perception and communication that women always are missing, or needing something: more training, more education, whatever that can be created to delay their leadership opportunity. Male colleagues may not have such stipulations; in fact, on more than one occasion I have witnessed post-placement training opportunities. Sometimes the woman who was passed over is the one responsible for training or 'getting them up to speed' or being their assistant that does all the work for which their boss takes or gets credit. This sets up a conflicted existence for aspirant women leaders as they also need to learn how to hurdle or circumvent existing barriers, jump through hoops placed in front of her within leadership culture to advance.

If the woman undertakes that requirement it causes her to lose an additional 2-4 years or more before she can be 'considered' for promotion opportunity. There are certainly companies that fund new leader or manager development opportunities focused on the skills needed for the position. I am not focused here on these. It is more so that some individuals get the leadership position and have the option of support to learn as they lead, while women or others are expected to have completed their learning prior to being considered for a leadership position. For women then, once the degree is completed, it means that their 'eligibility' for promotion is just beginning. Her counterpart would already have two more years' experience, as she now waits her turn for consideration. It can also mean that they are passed over in the interim for someone less qualified or who does not have that requirement. This signals that the intent to promote may never have been there, but that the delay for, or lack of, promotion is justified based on the stated need that candidates require an earned degree.

I note here that in the chapter on women's leadership effectiveness it was established that women have out-earned their male colleagues in terms of degrees over the past two decades, but the numbers in top leadership positions remain static and intractable, as the promotions do not always materialize. When this scenario is repeated more than once, peers and colleagues will recognize what is going on. They either take a cynical approach to the reality of inequity and remain silent about the inequities particularly if they are recipients of benefits while unqualified. Onlookers may also work to keep those who are qualified out of any possible promotion opportunities that could possibly threaten their aspirations. Remember too that the woman would also be economically hampered in this scenario. Managers are often quite willing to have conversations that 'pick a subordinate's brain' or to cull ideas from the woman's creativity and intelligence or place them on committees for their knowledge and wisdom, yet never once consider them sufficiently prepared for the leadership position their work sustains or promotes. This sends disconfirming messages and can affect employee morale because the feeling of being used lingers long after the incidents have passed.

The Spin of Women's Weakness. Another pervasive spin with consequences on women's leadership is the claim of their weakness. Remember that culture drives much of our worldview and the way we look at things. Culture also constructs the systems that show which frames will hold the spin. Here's what I mean. When cultures are open to following and accepting alternative facts, the public and the media can become unable to recognize truth, competence, and reality when they see it in front of them. Discernment and critical thinking ability are compromised by the preconceived perceptual framework that has been shaped with the prevailing narrative which results in closing off individuals from to recognition of other viable options presented to them. Drop that into leadership culture, and the spin of women's weakness becomes linked to women's generally smaller size and build which is conflated with the perception that she is not strong enough or not competent enough to lead. Women are highly productive working hard at work and at home. There is deceptive strength and power in women's capacity, productivity and competency, if they can be productive in the midst of hostile contemporary leadership context and the culture of silence. In keeping with the upcoming case study of what can happen when a woman for the first time seeks a top leadership position in a historically male-dominated environment. The weakness spin continues to block women's social mobility and self-determination and access top leadership positions. It belies any strength not physically or authoritatively shown and mischaracterizes other forms of leadership strength demonstrated.

Another layer of this spin is in relation to women's weakness in terms of physical capacity. This is a projection of the physical stamina that a woman may have as it relates to the workplace, and by extension a gibe at the woman's ability to lead. Arguably, in terms of brute strength, many women are not as physically strong as men, though some may be. However, leadership is *not* always primarily based on physical strength. Speaking of strength, anyone who can sustain carrying 20-30 pounds for six or more months, as women do when they are pregnant, at a most basic level it refutes the notion of weakness. Here's why I say this. Many women carry this weight while continuing to fulfil work, marital, and relationship responsibilities. This is a physical capacity unique to women which for which leaders exploit and punish them. As I have described in Volume 1, exploitation comes in the form of economic abuse that can take the form of 1) no paid family leave at a time when it is most needed, 2) leaking or pushing women are out of the promotion pipeline at this critical time, 3)not hiring them because of pregnancy, 4) letting women go, 5) not reemploying them after family leave, or bringing them back to positions which cause them to lose ground in terms of career advancement opportunities. All the while denying bias and discrimination based on gender and touting diversity initiatives to attract the same talent that continues to be mistreated. Women lead in the workplace, then go home to lead and manage their spouses and families if they have children, they also may function as caregivers of parents. All roles that are not for the faint of heart. These spins are cultural and based on physical, cultural and even religious beliefs, though such beliefs have not taken into consideration women's intellect, physical competency and leadership capability. Then there's one more spin which has to do with credibility and trustworthiness.

The Spin of Untrustworthiness

Untrustworthiness is one other spin that has become a metanarrative ingrained in leadership culture and continues to keep women out of top leadership positions. Here it's as if an accomplished woman who is competent, demonstrates leadership capacity and effectiveness is not credible or somehow cannot be trusted. Prevailing social role prescriptions and the status quo are at play here and can prevent women from being nominated for promotions. Women who show agentic traits, otherwise considered to be male characteristics can be seen as unappealing or cold, unemotional, and called Bitches. They are not trusted because they are functioning outside of socially prescribed roles, so negative names are ascribed to them. This can also become manipulative if managers and colleagues start out by calling the woman 'honey' 'sweetheart' or 'baby' which are terms of endearment and therefore unprofessional in the workplace setting whether coming from colleague or boss. These names can switch in a split second to nasty, bitch and other choice words, when the woman resists such unprofessional familiarity as in the catcalling on the street. Women who reject these names and insist on professional titles or bundaries can also command respect, or generate mockery and not being taken seriously. By the way, such name- calling does not exist for her male colleagues. This 'spin' is alive and well. With the advent of email, social media, electronic transactions, doing global business, we are borderless. There are no limits to the perpetrator's ability to repeat a spin, thus it is easily reinforced. The real truth is not always what goes viral, so women have had to find ways to protect their hard-wire to lead, their reputations and their career advancement from the constant assault of shaded truth resorting at times to defensive self-protective survival mechanisms.

Self-Protectiveness. Women who lead, from observation, conversation and experience learn to become self-protective. The double-standard that praises men on the one hand for sharing their vulnerability and authentic weaknesses quickly destroys a woman for any semblance of similar authenticity and vulnerability, while simultaneously vilifying them for not being warm enough, not smiling enough, or being too cold and reserved. This places women in a conflicted position that is rife with tension and stress. It creates a situation that feels like walking on eggshells or among landmines, never sure that she is doing the 'right thing' or what will come back to 'bite her'. The right thing is never clearly defined but remains just outside her reach no matter how much she is professionally prepared. Some women build a defensive protective wall around themselves (controlling their emotions and relationships) to be able to focus and be productive in hostile environments. This self-protective defense can be so formidable that it spills over into their private lives.

Shades of Truth and Abuse of Women

The second deeper level is the link of myth, spins and double-standards to abusive behavior in the workplace. Upcoming chapters will more specifically address the abusive links, but it would be remiss of me if I did not at least mention the abusive nature of myths and spins here. Recall that the purpose of creating the metanarrative or story by the individual, culture, or society about others is to gain or maintain privilege and power, to exert control over other individuals through setting behavioral expectations. In the workplace the leaders and managers intentionally engage these metanarratives because they want power and control over their subordinates in the workplace. When women are agentic or challenge the status quo the first and most frequent place managers go is the poor evaluations and insubordination. To establish a written narrative or record that contradicts her expertise or competency. This smear tactic is useful for two things. First, is to entrench and spread a limiting counternarrative about the woman that others see and act upon, sometimes without knowing her personally. Second, to create a legitimized way to justify not promoting her as she would then not be a 'good fit' for the company. Then there is the expectation that the individual being evaluated sign off on their negative evaluation. The myth and spin? The statement written or said, that the signature does not constitute agreement with what is written. Really? If the individual refuses to sign or wants to add their perspective to the evaluation it is called insubordination. And, there you have it.

One more insidious method of coercive control is also used that links to abusive behavior. It is gas lighting. Gas Lighting[22] is used for controlling others by shading or twisting the truth to sow doubt and elicit fear, psychological and emotional confused responses. Perpetrators use it in the workplace, in leadership and in life to. Abusive or manipulative leaders, managers, and spouses will use this mechanism of controlling, manipulative, coercive behavior on victim spouses, followers and employees. Behavioral characteristics include: 1) Lying and exaggerating 2) frequent repetition (of lies or some shade of truth they want the victim to believe or others to believe about her 3) escalation with challenges, escalating commitment or digging in the heels on a position even when proven wrong 4) wearing out the victim with constant harassment 5) forming a co-dependent relationship with threats and coercion in the manager and employee relationship 6) Giving false hope such as promised promotions that don't materialize, and 7) micromanaging or 'policing' an employee's work 8) domination and authoritarian commanding behavior. These behaviors are relentlessly employed to get the victim to fearfully comply. However, instead of gaining the desired compliance, the consequences of such abuse include low morale, decreased productivity, erosion of self-confidence, stifled creativity, increased stress, second-guessing, and constantly needing discernment for not believing lies as truth.

Leadership Implications and Conclusions

The implications for leadership culture is that shaded truth can have significant consequences. For example, Sire points out that the context has to be primed for the acceptance of shaded of truth. Well the workplace has been carefully and systematically primed for a long time. Sire points out "there have long been many stories, each of which gives its binding power to the social group that takes it as its own." This binding power creates a "a shift toward cultural legitimation" and "an incredulity toward metanarratives."[23] My takeaway is that women's underrepresentation in top leadership positions is perpetuated because existing leadership culture and context have succumbed to the binding power of the narrative that they have accepted about women's leadership ability. So, leadership practice, company culture, policy and systems are bound to operate within the constraints of the narratives. The false narratives are rife with myths and spins that negatively or untruthfully shape perception and responsive behavior to women's capacity, capability and readiness for top level leadership.

Shades of truth and the Double-standard

The myths, spins, and double-standards women face neatly fit into the organizational meta-narratives created, perpetuated and acted upon in contemporary leadership culture. When it comes to leadership, the influential relationship that the leader has with followers is founded on conceptual understanding of the strategic importance and trust in leader words and decisions for the benefit of the company or community. When organizations operate on false narratives and shaded truth, when the attitudes and perceptions are guided by myths and spins women's access to leadership positions can be severely limited. A summary of comparative double standard based on gender is outlined in Figure 11.1 below:

Female Leader/High Potential	Male Leader /High Potential
Gender Stereotypes (expectations or ought to be's) (Heilman, 2001)	
Communal: concern for others, sensitivity, warmth helpfulness and nurturance	Agentic: Confidence, assertiveness, independence, rationality, and decisiveness
Agentic Traits	
Women showing agentic traits, seen as unappealing or cold. Counter to gender role expectations; results in poor evaluations from male evaluators; especially male dominated work contexts.	Men showing agentic traits, seen as appealing, based on gender role expectations. Result in high evaluations in both male and female work contexts
Perceived Value	
Women are worth less, on average they are paid 24% less), Undervalued; under-represented; underpaid for similar work; get let go or shut down fast. Passes not easily given, glass-ceiling lack of access to promotions	Worth more; paid based on potential, overvalued; over-represented; overpaid; can get a pass quite easily for behavior or sub-par performance; or glass-escalator promotion opportunities.
Display of Anger & Authority	
Women who raise their voices in authority (command/ anger) are labeled as hysterical or emotional. When they demonstrate selfcontrol they are considered cold and unemotional (lacking)	Men who raise their voices are considered to be strong and authoritative. Displays of anger/emotions it is authentic - are tacitly sanctioned, and not labeled.

Transparency & Authenticity	
Women's transparency is perceived as weakness and can have lethal consequences for women. Women, tend to be selectively transparent, and that is turned against them.	Men's full transparency is perceived as authenticity and strength. Even if such transparency is behavioral practice that is way below standard.
Trustworthiness	
Women operating outside of gendered role expectations are considered to be untrustworthy. the required 'trust factor' (Not granted initially, and grudgingly earned for women; can be lost over time; usually not restored)'	Trustworthiness: Men are trusted even though their actions prove to be untrustworthy or against the interest of women. the required 'trust factor' (a given, but can be lost over time; returned after time for men)'
Competency	
Women's competencies or accomplishments are often dismissed or denied, perceived as if fabricated. They are expected to be competent, experienced and prepared. Requires or has a burden of proof. Never enough	Competency. Men are often promoted then either supported by competent women who were overlooked; or allowed to 'grow into the position" Proof of competency is not always required; Assumed though not present.
Standards	
Women are held to a very high standard for practice of leadership. Ignored or not praised for high competence, because it is after all the standard. Immediately dismissed ridiculed if not evident.	Men are held to a much lower standard of practice. When they show any semblance or approximation to that lowered standard, they are overly praised and celebrated as if it were a major accomplishment

Figure 11.1 Comparative Gender Double-Standard.

This is even though women may have demonstrated the required mental strength and agility, fluidity and flexibility in difficult dynamic situations or the ability to stand and lead severe mental pressure. It also has to do with power, presence, capacity and competence which are all qualities women embody. For instance, Chief Theresa Kachindamoto in Malawi is small in stature, but had such palpable power and presence emanating from her that she appeared taller than she was. Her leadership competence broke through generational paradigms and perceptions of the hundreds of thousands of people for whom she was responsible. Her capacity for leading in what was traditionally a man's world was equally indisputable. One of the reasons she was chosen was because of her authentic relational leadership style. Chief Theresa is feared as the first woman traditional chief of the Dedza district in Malawi responsible for several villages each with their sub-chief. Her word is not questioned without consequences. She supports the requirement of truth in practice with standards and holds her village chiefs accountable for required shifts in attitude, traditional cultural behavior and leadership practice. Her record of countercultural changes such as reducing the incidence of child-marriages, a focus on girl's education and reforestation initiatives make her a legend and are a testament to her leadership effectiveness and competence.[24] The materiality of leadership moves beyond image and gender to personal and positional authority and competence demonstrated over time.

A theme that ran through the research is that pioneer women executives must prove they can lead, and that often means that they adopt masculine behavioral criteria to prove they are for real leaders. The expectation to become more like men in their behavior is contrary to women's natural behaviors. This expectation can place undue burden on women to be other than who they are naturally. The perceptual spin, narrative, and mental model operating in this expectation are driven by traditional cultural role prescriptions and include the perceptions that 1) men's forms of leadership are best because that's what we are familiar with, or how it's supposed to be. While there are similarities in the leadership styles both men and women use, women have their distinctive skills and preferences which have proven to be beneficial to the organizations they lead. 2) Women's having to lead like men to be effective has been disproven by research and statistics that support the opposite.

Women can and should lead authentically, using their own mix of skills and competencies for the benefit of the companies. What then is the problem? From my viewpoint, society and the workplace have come well past the first and second generation of women leaders in practice, but not in the mental models that continue to shape leadership culture and practice. I believe it is time to reframe the operating paradigms to align with the reality of women in the workplace, women as leaders and women's leadership effectiveness. Leadership context and culture has significantly changed, and it is time that workplace attitudes and behaviors catch up with the change in culture and context. Leaders need to lead the way of change. The duty of incumbent leaders, through leadership development, succession planning initiatives, and awareness is to be open to moving beyond the limitations of prevailing mental models.

Leaders have an open and ongoing invitation to initiate strategies that develop female high-potentials for the future benefit of the companies they run. Aspects of leadership practice that need to change: 1) Accepting women as effective transformational and democratic leaders. 2) Stop perceiving women's collaborative, communal, relational skills as weak but as a premium in a global environment. 3) Start depicting women who display any semblance of anger as being passionate and authoritative like other male leaders as opposed to being perceived or seen as emotional or hysterical. 4) That women being serious is more suited for leadership than is the expectation to smile, always be a pleasant team player to appease or appear non-threatening to those around her. Her male colleagues don't have this burden, neither should she. It is a workplace after all. 7) Recognizing and finding ways to change into fair practice the status quo of conspiratorial behavior, a misogynistic patriarchal social system that seeks to retain control at any cost rather than blaming women for their under representation. 8) That leaders in leadership practice admit that leadership as practiced is not what it is cooked up to be, honest enough about what is happening to do something about it. 9) Reducing the economic and personal cost for women who are hard-wired to lead by eliminating victim blaming, the wage gap, and loss of ground, by ensuring that women's career paths are cleared from systemic potholes and silencing tactics because women will not just disappear nor will they be silent.

My recommendations for change to occur is that leaders can begin with identifying and bringing clarity and awareness of the silence surrounding women's representation in top leadership positions. Leaders will need to push to also address gatekeepers of the narratives and story-tellers so that the myths of weakness, the spins of leadership effectiveness, untrustworthiness, and readiness to lead are all seen for what they are: deceptions that use false narratives to keep women out of top leadership positions and limit their advancement. Instead leaders as social architects must reconstruct or craft truth narratives that accurately reflect women's leadership effectiveness, their competence and capability to lead. The focus on truth is crucial because it appears that culture is increasingly open to accepting myths spins and outright lies as part of the fabric of our culture. Even if truth is disruptive, tell it anyway, because integrity is the guardrail of truth and authenticity. Truth is the light

Even if silence seems the better option to take, that silence must be broken if change is to occur. I believe, and one of my mantras is 'when good is silent then evil thrives.' It is why I write about the code of silence as being problematic. Here it is not just that silence sustains and perpetuates the myths and spins. It is also about the consequences to women who don't talk or if they are silenced or dismissed when they do speak, then narratives can be repeated, and abuse perpetuated. We delved into some of the metanarratives that cause silence or which are dependent on the silence for their continued existence. However, I believe if the wrong of persistent women's underrepresentation is to be made right then, as Ida B. Wells states, "light needs to be shed on the mistruths that serve to sustain the phenomenon and the perceptions inherent in the status quo."[25] The spotlight serves to illuminate the mistruths and related perception paradigms, and helps leaders, who ordinarily would dismiss the truth of women's leadership effectiveness to see clearly and act or respond to women's leadership aspirations in a better way.

As women, when you know the truth of who you are, you do not have to believe what people tell you about your capability, capacity and leadership effectiveness. Lead confidently in your hard-wired truth rather than succumb to the metaphors that are presented about your leadership and career advancement until the truth becomes your reality. It is the power to stand or operate in the tension between your present situational reality (what others say you are supposed to be) and your hard-wired reality (what you are becoming) until both come into alignment. Women do not have to accept an untrue story, if you know your truth just live it -and lead when opportunities present themselves. If you are truly hard-wired to lead it will show up regardless of what others say or even feel. The foundational purpose for highlighting and removing the myths, spins and shades of truth is that they form the bricks from which the various barriers against women are constructed. These bricks will have to be deconstructed to remove the barriers and reconstructed with truth as central to the narratives surrounding women's leadership. To understand how the barriers operate systemically and perceptually researchers have proposed several relevant metaphors to explain what happens with women in leadership practice and these will be described in the upcoming chapter.

Precís

This chapter examined truth from a postmodern perspective; the power and purpose for developing metanarratives particularly those that are shades of truth; and how silence can be both the facilitative protector and a consequential outcome of narratives that are acted on. The methods and conditions that predispose groups and societies to accept the story or metanarrative were outlined, and the underlying power play and quest for control by the storyteller or dominant groups over the people who accept and believe it. Shades of truth, myths and spins specific to women's persistent under-representation in top leadership positions were identified; and how they collectively serve to shape the narrative of women's leadership and serve to perpetuate the persistent underrepresentation in top leadership positions.

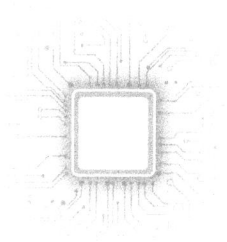

CHAPTER 12

Metaphors For Framing Women's Leadership Experiences

No country can ever truly flourish if it stifles the potential of its women and deprives itself of the contributions of half of its citizens."_ Michelle Obama

Women's leadership challenges continue to baffle researchers, scholars and theorists and women who want to lead. Scholars and theorists have resorted to the use of metaphors to try to figure out and explain what might be going on, when women face social, political, and economical constraints in fulfilling their intellectual, and emancipatory goals. Goals for leadership and career advancement all have these constraints. The phrases and concepts that follow are, at face value, unrelated to women's leadership. Yet, they plausibly conceptualize the persistent under-representation of women in top leadership positions which is so obvious that scholars and leadership thought leaders have identified these metaphoric phrases that we can relate to, to facilitate our understanding of what might be occurring.

The metaphoric descriptors are simultaneously simple and nuanced methods for communicating the complexity in the experiences of women that are more common than we care to admit in organizations. Yet, these are also workplace experiences and practices that some leaders and businesses would rather not see changed – at least not yet. The descriptors I will address include 'silencers,' 'lines,' 'glass ceilings,' 'labyrinths,' 'pipe-lines,' 'glass cliffs,' 'egg-shells,' and 'sieves.' This chapter will focus on these descriptive metaphors to assist with understanding what undergirds the persistent under-representation of women at the highest levels of leadership.

Victim Silencers

In chapter nine on the code of silence, I used the metaphor of gun silencers[1] as a powerful and useful descriptor for understanding and recognizing what has been and is happening in relation to women's access to top leadership positions. I point out there that high potential women are subject to organizational 'sniper attacks' with silencers which confuse the victim and investigators of the 'crime' as to the source and direction of the problem. It was noted that male (and sometimes female) counterparts could be the solid objects which serve to confuse the direction of the sniper-attacks -wittingly or unwittingly. The contemporary leadership culture is a context ripe for such behavior because of patriarchal tendencies, gender role prescriptions, and the silence that surrounds the experiences of women who have been silenced on their way to the top. The silence of the sniper means they must compartmentalize, can be removed, distracted by the confusion as to the originator; or there is collusive silence by those in the know; and of course, the silence of the women who are taken out -no longer able to speak up on their behalf. Other metaphors are quite simple.

The Line

About a century before most of these metaphoric descriptors were proposed, and way before the word suffrage became a household word, Harriet Tubman, a woman of color and slave aptly and simply described additional limitations placed on women of color's career advancement and professional self-determining aspirations. Tubman captured her observed experience with this statement: "In my mind, I see a line, over that line, I see green fields and lovely flowers and beautiful white women with their arms stretched out to me over that line, but I can't seem to get there no how. I can't seem to get over that line."[2] There are two salient aspects of this line for women's access to leadership opportunity that readers need to keep in mind. First, that there is distinction between the experiences of equally qualified and competent black women and white women and that challenges inherent to access to key positions in leadership for women of color are greater in the workplace or in any area of life they wish to pursue.[3] Second, it sets up the myths and spins in the organization that are dependent for their effectiveness on the ability of leadership culture to maintain and or move the line further away if too many women of color come close to it in professional practice. The shades of truth that are promoted consciously or unconsciously are key sources of implicit and explicit bias, which play a role in moving that line of rewarded accomplishment further away each time it is approached by too many women, or women of color. Once women approach the line, it is as if they are blocked or caught on a path with a dead-end as in a labyrinth.

The Labyrinth

The metaphor of a labyrinth was proposed by Eagly & Carli to describe the challenges encountered all along the way of women's advancement to leadership positions. As indicated previously, if 40% of women are in managerial and only four percent make it to the C-Suite what happens to the other 36% of women?[3] A Labyrinth is characterized by passages that are irregular, with difficult networks, secret passages; and many dead ends. The labyrinth, because of its characteristics is filled with distractions, delays and timewasters as a result of going down the wrong road. Inevitable detours result from having gone down the 'wrong path'. Hoyt,[4] for example, presents 1) human capital such as education, training and work experience, 2) gender differences in leadership style, effectiveness and agentic traits deemed important for top leadership positions and 3) prejudice based on gender stereotypes and biases as three categories that make up the labyrinth.

Many of the arguments posed in 1 and 2, are no longer true because women are increasingly agentic in terms of human capital and their leadership styles have been proven effective. Additionally, women are currently outpacing their male counterparts in educational preparation, leadership development, and make up a substantive number in the workplace, but changes in perception and expectations for them in leadership practice has not kept pace with those changes. Yet the prejudices, bias and gender stereotypes still hold sway in workplace for top-leadership selection practices and continue to keep numbers of women represented persistently low. Although it has improved slowly over time, there is something wrong with the systems that somehow causes women to lose their place when they are next in line for leadership positions.

The Pipeline Metaphor.

The pipeline is another metaphor that is used in relation to women's leadership. Not in terms of effectiveness alone, but also in terms of why the numbers remain at the low 4% for such a long time. The significance of this metaphor is because it is also used as a model for succession planning in companies.[5] This immediately places the underrepresentation of women in top leadership positions as a failure in succession planning for every organization where it exists. Let's explore why this is important. One of the primary concerns for oil companies are breaks or ruptures in the pipelines carrying the oil. As the oil leaks out so does the potential revenue of the company that owns the pipeline and the profits of their stakeholders. The major stakes for companies lies not only in the volume and extent of the spills, but because of the significant economic losses and long-term environmental damage implicated. Depending on how large the leak is and how long it takes for the disaster to be discovered and stopped makes all the difference in the ultimate financial losses of the company.[5] These leaks can occur above ground or underground on land or in the sea. The ones that occur underground or in the sea are harder to identify, take longer to detect, and can occur for a while before, and sometimes after they are discovered because of their location and difficulty in figuring out how to plug the leaks.

In the organization, the 'draining' of women from leaky organization pipelines leading to the C-Suite positions has been occurring for decades with seemingly little focused attention to ensuring change. The size of the leak is directly proportional to the evident lack of women at the C-Suite level. If research and scholars, who have studied this phenomenon, persistently present women in leadership positions (CEO, president, board) as beneficial to company decision-making and bottom line. Then by extension, not only is the leak quite large, but it has largely been ignored, gone undetected, or deliberately been allowed to continue as it has been ongoing for several decades. While there has been no clear evidence that organization actuaries have spent time quantifying the financial risks of keeping women out of leadership positions, the connection between women's leadership and profitability suggests that such a focus in leadership practice, might be a paradigm-changing and lucrative eye-opener.

Perhaps this is the inference behind the pipeline's becoming a metaphor for what is happening to women who aspire to lead in organizations. Women start out wanting to lead, as Fels points out, but are somehow shifted out of the leader track, overworked, out-networked, underpaid, un-sponsored, ignored and side-lined from their original goals.[6] The leaks went largely undetected for what they was for some time, hidden behind the various rationales proffered by a leadership culture that did not want women included. Like actuaries, research analysts and scholars have studied the problem and debunked the prolific justifications. Why? To highlight the risk to companies in a patriarchal society where culture, religion, schools and the workplace practice all are premised on women's subjugation, control, pay inequity, domination, and barriers to women's opportunities for advancement. Oil companies employ insurance actuaries, whose sole purpose is to analyze, calculate, and translate into dollars the probability of losses from a given incident using those statistics to calculate insurance risks. Think about that for a moment. I do believe there are actuaries in the workplace that serve a similar role as the actuaries in the oil or insurance industry in their statistical analysis of risk. These actuaries do exist in companies with a role to calculate the amount of insurance money needed to silence women employees who raise discrimination, sexual harassment and pay inequity issues and cover the company's true reputation.

There is a strong correlation between leadership culture and oil companies in this instance. Both corporations and oil companies employ risk assessors who are retained more to support the company in providing the insurance payouts than the money to fix the pipe-line or organizational 'accidents' such as non-promotion or salary inequities. Insurance to mitigate the risk and cost of women who might seek legal recourse for discriminatory behaviors, pay and actions is available. But the steps to create a leadership culture where such actuarial activities are unnecessary, or where analytic decisions made to benefit one group are also expected to benefit all groups and ultimately the company are still lacking. The tactic here is to respond purposively to the research and statistical findings which show that companies with women in top leadership positions and on Boards show increased profitability, revenue, better decision making, and are ultimately more competitive.[7] The reasonable goal would be to take conscious steps to develop women positioning them for developmental opportunities that move them up the career advancement line. Leadership culture would ensure that women are neither forgotten, side-lined, or passed over when promotion opportunity comes. This will take a concerted effort by all. Why? Because women *and* men have bought into the current system of leadership culture and practice in society. Any change will have to have the collaboration of everyone to bring the needed changes of the system to fruition. We're at the place where such action needs to be taken. The pipeline is explicitly linked to workplace upward mobility, this invisible but tangible barrier for women has also been called the glass ceiling.

The Glass Ceiling

The persistent reality is that women have not been able to attain leadership positions at the rate one would expect given their numeric presence in the workplace. Olsen & Walker point out, "while the number of women entering management positions slowly continues to increase; women remain underrepresented at the senior executive level."[7] One of the early metaphors used to explain this reality is the glass ceiling. Lampe defines it as the "invisible, yet quite impenetrable, barrier that serves to prevent all but a disproportionate few women from reaching the highest ranks of the corporate hierarchy, regardless of their achievement and merits."[8] It is such a pronounced trend, and has been so clearly evidenced across industries and business sectors alike, the inequities so pronounced, that the term "glass ceiling" has been metaphorically used to describe the phenomenon.

In organizations, these tacit expectations can also influence the perceptions of who could (or should) lead. Hoyt points out "not only are the decision makers influenced by the stereotypes that disadvantage women in a leadership role, but they may succumb to homosocial reproduction, a tendency for a group to reproduce itself in its own image."[4,8] What this means is that the good old boys club still only wants boys in the club or what is called replicating homogeneity. The house is built for men, it is a place where women are marginalized - not a place where women can fully thrive because it is not yet structured to include them.

The time came in 2008, and again in 2016 for the United States of America to come face to face with the historic reality of a woman as President, and the time has gone without a woman being selected. The glass ceiling had 18 million cracks[9] in 2008 years ago, and 2.8 million more votes than the current president earned in the 2016 election. But, as of this writing the glass ceiling for women at the highest position in the nation remains a cracked but unshattered barrier. Now, there was incremental and historical progress made as the candidate became the first-time female nominee of a major party ever. Yet, as is common in the workplace when competent and capable women are passed over, the candidate is blamed for somehow inexplicably falling short of vague or unspecified requirements.

This barrier is also present if a woman steps out from under the company's auspices to lead her own company and becomes an entrepreneur.[10] As the leader of the company, besides facing similar barriers in the external environment, there is also another glass or invisible but tangible barrier she faces. The invisible barrier this time is access to investor funds to help make her company successful, where she is inexplicably denied for unspecified reasons funds that are available to her male counterparts. By using glass for the ceiling, the metaphorical illustration of the glass ceiling[11] is that it is tangible to its victims but can be simultaneously invisible. At times women who break through the glass ceiling or make it through the labyrinth might find themselves facing another form of invisible barrier, or what some have called the glass cliff.

The Glass Cliff Metaphor

The *Glass Cliff* metaphor the sad reality of this metaphor speaks to one of the barriers addressed that stops highly qualified women from willingness to step in' or 'accept' senior leadership positions. It is a precarious situation where "women more likely… rise to positions of organizational leadership in times of crisis than in times of success, and men more likely to achieve those positions in prosperous times."[12] It is when companies or countries are in trouble that they tend to seek out a woman or person of color. Human tendency is to forget or to glorify those who were once vilified. The vision of danger conjured up by the glass-cliff visual is very real. The stakes are high, the risks are great; the blame easy if things aren't turned around. The leader needs to put in place the guardrails that will halt the precipitous downward slide; and will also need to install stopgaps that will help them pull the company back up and away from the edge. The process is a difficult and complex one.

Women who have led on the glass cliff, are chosen to lead companies or countries that are in deep trouble. Here's what I mean. The NAACP elected its first female CEO when the company or institution is trying to 'save their brand.' Similarly, as in the Baylor University case, the institution sought to appease major constituents (women and students) and contributors to their financial efficacy after major sexual violence scandal by hiring a female president. Finally, the United Kingdom (UK) elected Theresa May as Prime Minister in the wake of the chaotic political environment which resulted in the Brexit vote. The people voted a very close decision to withdraw from the European Union (EU), but there was no plan. The consequences of this decision are unknown, and the UK does not fully know the impact this economic decision will have on the country's future economic viability and survival. The Parliament has to date not been able to come to consensus on several plans and exit options that Theresa May negotiated with the EU. But both May, and the country, teetered on the edge of the glass cliff without the safety net or guard rails of an executable plan to withdraw from the EU, until she resigned. There is currently no concrete plan, even with the new prime minister in place.

This metaphoric phenomenon or leadership practice is identified because of its noted pattern. The glass cliff makes leadership an exceptionally dangerous high-risk prospect for the woman leader, especially since her leadership effectiveness is (quite often) linked to the company's success. The double-bind here is first, that in such dangerous situations men tend to step back, or the people choose the woman to save the day. However, when the woman turns that company around and it is again successful, there is movement for the same woman to be ousted by selecting another male -now that the company is doing well.[12]

Going back to the Speaker of the House for a moment, now that she has tactically and painstakingly laid the groundwork and delivered the House of Representatives with a decisive democratic majority and an unprecedented number of women representatives the immediate discussion focused on who would challenge her for the leadership position I believe she earned.[13] It is as if some are unwilling to allow her to lead what she had successfully built. It makes no real sense given that there is no better candidate to lead the House, strategically and transactionally than the one who built it in the current climate. Pelosi also is an example of the metaphor that follows as in leading in an egg-shell environment. The classic illustrations of glass-cliff leadership metaphors are inclusive of a recognition which suggests that a more strategic, relationship-oriented leadership is needed crisis situations. Ordinarily the woman would not have this opportunity to lead, but in this instance, send in the woman, let's see what she can do to fix the situation. No man wants to take the job because of the high risk. The reasoning behind such action seems to stem from 1) it is already a crisis, so give her a try. I don't want this connected to my name. 2) It is a no-win high-risk situation and she might fail anyway, setting up a self-fulfilling prophecy. 3) women are good at solving difficult workplace problems – a major unconscious bias which should translate into more of their leadership but doesn't. Bruckmuller and Brascombe's[14] perspective is that when there is more likely an opportunity for success, men get appointed; when there is more likely opportunity for failure (or if the company is already failing) women are appointed. This is of course a stereotypical choice response. The upside?

Women can and have demonstrated they can handle tough situations and potentially change the minds of men who expected them to fail. The downside is a discriminatory, gendered perspective that causes women's leadership talent to be lost in successful companies and men's talent in crisis. We don't get to see enough women leading in successful companies but women are deemed better able to handle crisis. Why this holds women back is because, if things appear to be fine in the company, they are not ordinarily considered for leadership positions. Crisis forces decision-makers to think out-side the box of the status quo and to see women's leadership capacity with new eyes. Kenny Roger's song *the Gambler* has two lines that hold salient meaning for women who lead on the glass cliff "You've You got to know when to hold 'em, know when to fold 'em, know when to walk away and know when to run."[15]

Women in glass-cliff leadership positions need to constantly keep monitoring their status as leader, their ability to lead effectively, and the strength or support of their followership. Speaker Pelosi is holding 'em and remains on the glass cliff as leader of the House of Representatives and may well end up as President if the current administration continues on the path to destroy all protective guard rails of governmental norms of practice. Prime Minister May has walked away by resigning her position, since every deal option she negotiated has been rejected and the country seems bent on going off the cliff without safeguards. She perhaps is running from being the first to go over the edge in a possible 'hard Brexit' which may be a wise thing to do -who knows. Now that May negotiated three deal options and won EU time and concessions for the country to decide their course in an organized and planned way, the men lined up to take the position no one wanted a couple years ago, when the people decided and they had no plan. The leader who originally promoted Brexit, now has full responsibility and accountability for executing his original plan -if he can. To date the jury is still out, as no plan is in place. There is one more metaphor that relates more to the internal reason for the bias and barriers against women's leadership and advancement. It has to do with the mindsets, mental models, worldviews and perceptions which serve as a filter or sieve in the decision-making process.

Leading in Egg-Shell Environments

The egg-shell phenomenon points to another metaphor for women's leadership context. As mentioned in the previous section, the difficult cultures and contexts some women lead in can be fragile and dangerous. This woman has to be exceptionally careful with her every move for 1) fear she will break fragile relationships or some norm she has not been told about, 2) fear of letting others down or working with those who want her to fail, 3) fear that she would be considered by others to have 'dropped the ball' or not have met expectations which were not clearly outlined, and 4) fear of being dependent on those who do not want her leadership for evaluation of her performance, which may mean she cannot do anything right from their perspective. The basis of this metaphor is fear and the emotional labor requirement to be overly cautious is quite high. The consequences are isolation, stress, lack of trust, emotional abuse, and being excluded from critical network groups. The context is one where there is a lot of politics and in-fighting for power to control turf or one where others look to hold something over her for future favors. It can be in a context where or she knows there are powerful enemies around or working for her. The relationships are at arms-length so she can protect herself from those who are perceived or known to be looking for any opportunity to destroy her. I believe that contemporary examples include Theresa May, Nancy Pelosi, or women who are pioneer leaders in male dominated sectors who are expected to prove leadership capacity in crisis or hostile environments. These leaders all must develop and master relational and transactional skills and overcome the preconceived notions of what a leader in charge should look or be like all at the same time.

The Deceptive Sieve of Mental Models

The metaphors up to now (glass ceiling, glass cliff, pipe-line, labyrinth, gun-silencer and line) were focused on explaining the experiences and challenges of women in the workplace. These metaphors point to the systems and processes that result in the intractable one to four percent statistic of women in top leadership positions. The sieve metaphor, on the other hand, explains why women have these challenges and experiences. The root cause of women's workplace challenges is a powerful sieve of "mental models" which have ability to destroy all change initiatives or potential opportunities for improvement in leadership practice. According to Senge, mental models are "deeply held internal images of how the world works, images that limit us to familiar ways of thinking and acting."[15] Mental models speak to why the numbers and experiences of 80- 90% of women who may want a leadership opportunity still don't motivate leader's action to change it. No amount of understanding that results in change is possible if the perceptual frameworks, or 'mental models' are not addressed.

The powerful significance of mental models is that they also can be diametrically oppositional to data, statistics, workplace practice, professional preparation, outcomes evidence and people's characteristics that contradict them. The purpose of the sieve is to block the passage of unwanted particles based on things like size and shape. In this case, women are blocked from getting through, trapped and their passage into the desired final product or position in this case. What would ordinarily be easily allowed through for the benefit of the company (needed leadership skills and abilities) is blocked because it does not fit the hole(s) of prevailing mental models of leadership. Only things that fit the cultural narrative, the status quo or the prescribed perception, is allowed to filter through.

In talking about perception, we have moved from the objective to the subjective aspects that drive the decision-making behaviors. And, when subjectivity is part of our decision heuristic, it's easy to fall into the perception trap. The larger part of leadership decisions, management hiring practices are driven by mental models, which influence perception, and ultimately the subjective decision to select leaders based on the 'flesh' of embodied leadership -which is both intuitive and subjective.[16] Here's how the body taps into intuitive and subjective decision-making. Bordo points out that the body functions as a 'carrier-metaphor' for all the negatives and positive perceptions of competence, capacity, capability for leadership – in the minds of selecting committees, and identification of future leaders. Bordo goes on to describe the body as a text or metaphor of culture: prevailing and enforced cultural notions of gender differences are inscribed on the body, as it shapes itself to fit conventions of proper appearance, deportment and physical activity.[17] The culturally inscribed limits of that body are also the perceptual limits placed on or ascribed to that person in relation to their perceived capability.[18] So, the paradox for women who lead is that women's bodies simultaneously communicate expectations of women in the language of the culture (femininity and acceptable of non- leader gender-based roles) and also characteristic expectations of men (masculinity and acceptable performance in the role as leader). This embodied paradox disrupts cultural and leadership conventions, and challenges prevailing mental models and behavioral practices in organizations which still continue to operate by the original traditional (or patriarchal) conventions. This is what traps decisionmakers.

The Perception Trap

The perception trap lures and catches us, and before we know it we are caught and can't get out. Unless we are vigilant enough to identify the snares, threads, or ropes, wires of the trap and avoid them we are inevitably caught up in them. The salience of this metaphor is borne out in the leadership practice data and the peculiar silence that protectively shields the behaviors behind the codes. Perception, then, is influenced by biases, emotions, cultural readiness; and based on six senses: touch, sight, taste, smell, hearing and proprioception, or the "set of senses involving the ability to detect changes in body positions & movement" For instance, familiar differences between women and men, cognitive processing of information, how we sense and interpret reactions, tone of voice, image, and recognize behavioral patterns and familiar or unfamiliar categories. The sieve metaphor makes it clear how a person can engage in selective perception and it becomes easier to understand how selective perception can occur. Only what fits the need for consistency with the mental model or only what can pass through the perceptual framework or sieve holes, is seen. Other factors are ignored or dismissed if they interfere with the decision-makers wishes, cognitions, or belief systems. Additionally, mental models come with their own selective perception and 'perceptual defenses"[19] or protective blinders that keep the person from recognizing how different, or inconsistent data that presents itself against what the mental model would suggest can actually be relevant. The automatic defenses show up when the person is feeling cognitive dissonance and person blocks it out because of anxiety, discomfort, or fear. The perceptual defenses prevent the person's progress toward 'Perceptual Readiness' which keeps the person from being open seeking out other options. In this instance, the individual holds very strongly to what they know and are not open to seeing how a broader perspective can be better or more helpful. The prevention of readiness is based on the individual's needs, values, cultural background, personal interests and openness to change. [19]

For instance, if the leader is male and wants homogeneity in the C-Suite as has been the status quo because he is more comfortable that way. When a qualified woman applies for a C-Suite position, he or the selection committee will want to reject the application because perceptual defenses would prevent him from seeing the skills and competencies she brings to the table. Ordinarily the leader would have selected a similarly qualified person -if they were male. Being a female with these qualifications is so different it causes anxiety and discomfort. Instead of acknowledging and addressing the cognitive dissonance, the immediate reaction is to activate the perceptual defenses which would result in seeking reasons to disqualify or not hire her. The rationale would be framed by subconscious cultural socialization, reinforcement from other male executives, or traditional leadership practice which would block any openness or movement toward being ready to examine or deal with the perceptual inconsistency of hiring a woman with leadership capacity for the first time. In fact, such a woman, when she applies for top leadership positions is perceived as forward, presumptuous or too ambitious. The woman's actions can infuriate and upset the norm by providing data that is clearly contrary to biased expectations and practice. The result is the woman's application is not taken seriously. A male counterpart would be chosen ahead of the woman simply because decision makers can better defend the justification for denial, than their not being 'ready' to proactively justify the first-time choice to select the qualified woman. So, the cycle continues.

Conclusion and Leadership Implications

The metaphors discussed in this chapter have been presented to clarify understanding of what has continued to occur in the companies and countries for decades. Tubman's centuries-old description of a line as a barrier is deceptively simple. Yet it is quite clear in its explanation of the barrier facing women of color which often silently communicates you can go so far but no more. This 'line' is still clearly visible for women of color as the lack of women of color in top leadership positions continues to attest. The labyrinth, pipeline and gun-silencers, and glass ceiling as imageries of women's career advancement experiences. As metaphors they help us to examine the various challenges faced by women in the process of gaining access, the experiences and career advancement outcomes of many women who seek or aspire to lead. As they move in the direction of their leadership aspirations, the metaphors illustrate how they encounter problematic leadership and workplace systems and practices that are currently in place to slow down their progress.

The appearance is that the women are somehow lost, distracted, redirected, blocked and silenced in the quest for that top position in ways that are not experienced by their male counterparts. The contrasting metaphor used for male counterparts is a glass escalator. An invisible, smooth path to the top. When women finally attain the sought-after leadership position, the invisible challenges they face in these leadership opportunities can be captured in the metaphorical phrases 'glass cliff' and 'walking on egg-shells'. The former describes challenges, crises and complexity that may have opened up access to leadership for them, the latter highlights the existential danger or cost to women who may have finally been granted access. The glass cliff also speaks to the points in time when companies may be more open to granting women access to top leadership positions.

Beyond women's experiences in the quest for advancement, the metaphors further provide snapshots of company culture or the times when companies are more open to women as leaders. This includes times such as being on the brink of company failure or when the risk is so high that men don't want to be connected to it. In those situations, there is greater readiness or willingness to place a woman in leadership because it is a precarious position. This brings us to the final metaphor I mentioned for elucidating the experience. The mental models 'sieve'. From my vantage point it is by far the greatest deterrent of women's advancement to leadership positions and goes to the heart of the mindsets which shape worldviews, decision-making and behaviors. Mental models are what lead to the moral disengagement and a lack of personal accountability that results in transgressive behaviors which was discussed in Volume 1. Latham in the book *Work Motivation,*[19] suggests some practical ways leaders, CEO's and Boards can address and change the metaphors ascribed to the reality of women's leadership in organizations. Leaders can 1) constantly monitor and publicize corporate practices that have detrimental human and company effects. Such as addressing the absence of women from Board and top leadership positions in company practice and changing the context to one that is more inclusive. 2) Companies can increase the transparency of the discourse by which corporate policies and practices are formulated. For instance, being open to discussion and transparency around salary and wages to move toward an equity agenda with a goal of eliminating the wage gap. Or, discussing and changing hiring criteria and decision-making if it always results in not selecting women, or to meet the goals of inclusion. 3) Be diligent in exposing sanitizing language or false narratives that mask truth[20] such as moving the shades of truth into the light of honest scrutiny. In other words, call inappropriate behavior, unclear criteria and biased perceptions what they are: inappropriate and biased. Creating language to make what is wrong appear right or acceptable would no longer be needed.

Finally, the language of honesty can positively transform leadership culture into new metaphors which no longer illustrate the limiting experiences but also create unimpeded glass-escalator pathways of access to leadership opportunities for women. A key mechanism for making it past the metaphoric constraints is having vigilant sponsorship and appropriate support systems. One vital support system is the presence of other women in leadership or sisterhood (in or out of the organization) who can help aspiring women navigate the conflicted tension of the middle ground.

When a woman is operating in a workplace culture between limiting metaphors she can have a difficult time. The new metaphor she may be writing as an aspiring leader, with the support of others becomes an essential mechanism for achieving and sustaining access to leadership positions. The support can come in the form of having a community where the woman no longer has to be silent about her experiences, but able to talk about them and gain clarity about the context and how to best respond to presenting challenges. Leaders in their sphere of influence are also accountable for initiating change that is needed in every area where change is necessary. Change can also include working to eliminate selective perception. For instance, as leaders drop their perceptual defenses, they can lead and model the perceptual readiness that include equal consideration of women. Leaders would then be open to sponsoring high-potential women candidates or including them in projects where their leadership capability can be observed. Sustainable change here requires reframing the paradigms or mental models of gendered socialization and leadership capacity. The pipeline would no longer leak, the glass ceiling would be broken, there would be clear directions to navigate the labyrinth or a straight path, gun-silencers would be outlawed with transparency, and the line would be erased as women ride the glass escalator to the top alongside their male counterparts. There would be an irresistible and phenomenal pull beyond the perceived risk to the blessing of a strong bottom line, better decision-making and an inclusive leadership culture.

Precis

There have been several metaphors proposed in explanation of why more women are not in top leadership positions. The metaphors provide an account for the persistent and intractable paucity of highly competent women in the C-Suite. Descriptors include lines, glass-ceilings and glass cliffs signifying the tangible, but invisible hurdles and challenges faced to labyrinths, gun silencers and pipelines focused on the organizational processes and systems that block women's access to leadership opportunity. The final metaphor, the sieve, focuses on the perceptual defenses which only allow information which fits the mental models or paradigms. Perceptual readiness indicates the level of openness to new practices and ultimately influences the decision-making process. The key here is to understand the metaphors as leaders and to ensure that they are not played out as part of the systems of company leadership practice.

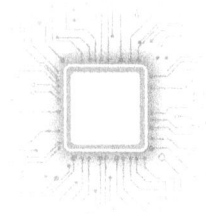

CHAPTER 13

Igniting A Revolution: A Case Study

"Do not go where the path may lead, go instead where there is no path and leave a trail." _Ralph Waldo Emerson

Trailblazing can be quite daunting. Pioneers choose to honor their hard-wire to lead or step up to leadership positions despite the obstacles set in their paths. Women's embrace of their greatness is continually contested in leadership culture. A special type of courage is required to go where others have not gone before, to face the leadership challenges of pioneers and trailblazers head on. There are a myriad of reasons for the challenges that can undermine a woman's innate desire and hard-wire to lead. Do the reasons truly speak to the under-representation of women in contemporary top leadership positions or to something else? Here we examine just a few of the challenges of women who are breakthrough leaders through the lens of the observed experience of the 2016 United States presidential race linking it to some of the myths, spins and social identity (gender) biases that played out or were evident in real-time. The chapter concludes with the powerful revolutionary cultural dynamism which was set in motion by the actions of a pioneer leader.

Journey Toward a Revolution

Hannah Arendt points that "in acting and speaking, [wo]men show who they are, reveal actively their unique personal identities and thus make their appearance in the human world, while their physical identities appear without any activity of their own in the unique shape of the body and sound of the voice."[1] Arendt' portrayal of who people are is distinct from their qualities, gifts, talents, and shortcomings. These unique identities, whether displayed or hidden, are foundational to what the person says or does. Clinton, the female candidate's leadership development journey began decades ago with the development of her gifts, acquiring knowledge, experiences, skills, and abilities which translated into a level of preparation and competency to a scale that few could match. Some of this experience and knowledge was developed as a First Lady (to a governor and a president), with a seat up close and personal to the position she would aspire to attain. Some experience was gained by positions held as lawyer, legal advocate, mother, U.S. Senator, and Secretary of State among others. The candidate's revolutionary journey was punctuated by relentless but unfruitful investigations, the impeachment of her husband and a losing bid for the democratic party nomination in 2008, to her opponent Barack Obama who would become the 44th President of the USA for the next eight years.[2] The campaign's approach held that the objective focus was to be on knowledge, experience and competency, but not overly on gender and history. From my standpoint the election experience served as a classic and sobering reminder that the barriers to women's leadership were, and are, still prevalent in business and public spheres.

The candidate's subsequent position as Secretary of State simultaneously acknowledged her remarkable leadership capability and competency, but also illuminated the significant barriers to women's leadership, the societal acceptance of her placement in a supportive role to the position that had yet to be won.[3] At this point, hope that the path to the Presidency would be possible remained alive. In 2016, after making groundbreaking history as the first woman ever to become a major party nominee in the country, and poised to shatter the metaphorical glass ceiling, the candidate was passed over once more. Subsequently, I heard reactions and rationalizations, familiar to me from organization contexts, surface as pundits sought to explain and understand what happened. Explanations ranged from lack of media coverage, to blame for not being a 'good' candidate, to those who knew the candidate was not going to win because she did not fight back hard enough, to not having articulated a clear message the spokes- people for the collective sought to articulate the shocking outcome of an operating system, Most analysts presented their reasons without making the key connection to the gender-biased patriarchal system, context and culture in which her bid was made, and not acknowledging their role in perpetuating the status quo leadership culture and practice.

The irony here is that the United States of America, historically considered to be the 'leader of the free world' still continues to lag behind other less developed or third-world countries and peer governments when it comes to women in top leadership positions. The historical progress made was incremental but very important for women. The candidate's nomination as the first female of a major party was historic on its own merits. Other women had competed for a bid for the nomination before, but none with the real sense of serious possibility that would push our culture to have to seriously consider and choose a woman as president. The election results in 2008 and in 2016 will continue to be a solemn reminder that the U.S., one of the leading countries in the global landscape that has fought for human and women's rights, will still need to consciously, tactically and strategically lift the cultural moratorium on women as leaders in this and other key positions just like corporations.

Creating a Revolutionary Shift in Culture

Cultural dynamism or cultural shift begins with the actions of leaders. The leader's action sets off a ripple effect or sets in motion a change movement that may be slow or swift but it is irreversible. At the nexus of the leadership, cultural and social discourse, a deeply fascinating and intriguing quasi-revolutionary leadership example publicly played out before our very eyes. In full disclosure, it is important to note that I am independent, non-party affiliated, but deeply interested in all things leadership. Women's leadership as a societal phenomenon in all its complexity fascinates and intrigues me. Nonetheless, a revolution is defined as "an overthrow or repudiation and the thorough replacement of an established government or political system by the people governed"[4] The quasi-revolutionary aspect under consideration is more benign than the definition describes and does not fulfil all the criteria, but I believe the effect may be the same. This definition includes the social aspects of a revolution that are more important for understanding the significance of women's leadership, and this case example. Any woman stepping into the top position as president of the United States would be creating: "A radical and pervasive change in society and the social structure, especially one made suddenly and often accompanied by violence."[4] It would be a fundamental and radical change in our society and social structure as indicated. Because, even though it is inevitable, it will take concerted radical learning, collective perspective and paradigm shifts by men and women for it to work in a patriarchal society, that still is not quite ready.

Aspects of the definition not met include the suddenly and accompanied by violence.

Women have been leading and or aspiring to equality and leadership positions for close to a century so when they accomplish it it will not have been sudden. Women achieving this top position does not have to be accompanied by violence, but based on the barriers highlighted in Volume 1, and the Electoral College (EC) system, the jury is still out. If the EC remains in force, at minimum it needs recalibration and realignment so that it more closely represents and aligns with the popular vote. I believe it did not represent the 'sense of the people' and that the EC failed in its analysis of the qualities adapted to the station or the office of the president. Furthermore, the EC appears to be functioning more like a tyranny of the minority, though it was established to prevent the tyranny of the majority.[5] The first woman president will certainly represent a radical and pervasive change in society and the social structure. The selection of a woman as president will certainly be a thorough more equitable reconstruction, rather than a full repudiation and replacement of the established government and political system by the people governed if it comes via an election. If she is appointed the circumstances may trigger all aspects of the definition.

The Major Candidates

In the descriptors of the candidates I will use just the last names to identification and the points raised most closely representing the relevant issues of the women's leadership context and culture. Candidate Sanders mounted a passionate campaign which resonated surprisingly with a broad segment of the population and drew followers of all ages frustrated with the social challenges and their declining quality of life.

The radical proposals for systemic change sounded great, though the reality of their achievement was less so, and questionable in terms of possibility. As a candidate, he was an Independent who switched parties to oppose the single woman candidate Clinton. He generated strong and growing interest which ultimately translated into an authentic movement but not the win or revolution it was often described. Passion for the social issues of the people, and the prospect of a better future ignited a groundswell of support by some who felt they were not being heard, the youth, the unemployed or underemployed.

The opposing-party's candidate Trump also claimed that his following was revolutionary. The anti-diversity, anti-immigrant, anti-establishment, nationalist approach, couched in inflammatory rhetoric was also passionate. The promise of changing long-term unemployment by a return to a past with jobs, now extinct, in the face of irreversible societal changes also became a strong rallying point. Neither male candidate clearly outlined policies to achieve the promises they made, and as men they fit the status quo leadership profile. Indeed, the passionate proposals seemed to sound great to their followers; but the policies were not presented in the practical context of how they could be accomplished with the routine obstructions to policy-making currently in place. It did not seem to matter. Certainly, some passionate followers, actually came perilously close to the very real violence often associated with revolutions, given that the zeitgeist, ethos, and climate were uniquely ripe for some sort of revolutionary transformation. In this illustration, both male candidates sensed and accurately pinpointed a readiness for radical change. However, it was the fact that Clinton was a woman, and the first woman to achieve serious consideration of her candidacy which was more closely representative of a revolution. With clear and well-thought out policy proposals, the only real revolutionary change was in the nation taking the unprecedented step of electing a woman. Ironically, both Sanders and Trump sought to dismiss and defeat the very person in whom the authentic revolution was embodied. Clinton's male opponents rightly discerned that they were on the verge of something new and momentous, but just her selection as nominee would be a significant departure from the political norm. Her rise to the top office in the country would be a challenge social norms and perceptions, and leadership practice with which America had become familiar. The American perception of leadership would have to change to include her.

Societal Systems and Women's Under-representation

As frequently occurs with search committees in businesses, the nation stopped just short of creating a different and more futuristic national history based on systems that are well worth reexamination. Here's what I mean. It's not just because the candidate ultimately did not win the election that these points are highlighted. Clinton won the popular vote by a clear and decisive vote of 2.8+ million votes *more* than her male opponent yet, the Electoral College granted the male candidate with the lower number of votes, the presidency. The experience still rankles with many voters because of how it happened. Some voters felt disenfranchised and that their vote did not count. It presents a challenge to the justice, fairness and efficacy of an election system that uses a representative Electoral College while claiming democracy because it disenfranchises voters in an ever increasing and unprecedented way. Clearly, much like leadership culture needs systemic and cultural reexamination and change, the political system, where the requirement for an electoral college system which disenfranchises millions of voters also needs re-examination and change. A closer look at the system's efficacy and currency, including scrutiny of such practices as the race being called before all the votes are in. This is an issue because it is not the first time that the election was given to somebody who lost the popular vote. Some would argue that this outcome is legitimate. I disagree for several reasons. The legitimacy of a presidency under these circumstances is always questionable, and the unfairness is starkly evident. Another issue is that the race is called before it is actually over a communication that some votes don't really matter. It is hard to imagine any other competition where the opposing team is awarded the win even though the other team ran up the score unless the winning team was disqualified for use of a banned substance -after the game and an investigation. So, why is it that practice acceptable for such an important position, unless someone wanted to control the outcome of the race regardless of the actual outcome?

How can such an unexamined system continue to be allowed in the political arena? What occurred in the election outcomes of 2016, would never happen in sports arena. Consider this for a moment. In chapter 8, from a socio-cultural perspective I raised Gannon's[6] use of the sport of football as a cultural metaphor for the United States. The systems strategies, team orientation, fan-base and competition are woven into the cultural system and socio-cultural norms. In football there may be comments (some negative) when one team runs up the score on the other team in the game. But I have never witnessed the umpires and officials huddle together and then grant the win to the team with the lowest score. The team with the highest score wins. Period. A popular vote of nearly three million more votes is akin to running up the score, yet the win was given to the candidate with the lower number of votes. In this instance the EC not only operated against the will of the people, but called the game before the final score was posted.

Drop this scenario into workplace practice and we find that corporate leadership culture, in some industries more than others, operates by what Trompenaars and Hampden-Turner, call an "error correcting system"[7] that political leadership culture can benefit from and perhaps adopt. Much like the routine calibrations of reagents, instruments and machines to ensure the repeated precision of their function, the error correcting system involves a process of reviewing errors or anomalies that occur, with an eye to "learning from error correction…or how particular exceptions are encountered."[7] They point out that "no scientific law can ignore mounting anomalies" and "no corporate procedures can fail to account for a growing number of exceptions."[7] More than one such occurrence is considered to be a crisis where "rules must be reformed or new ones created."[7] Well, the U. S. general elections has seen more than one anomaly involving the use of the EC over the years. And I wonder why its usefulness is not re-examined as similar errors in performance would be examined in other entities, and industries? The latest and most significant instance is one showing a much greater margin of error than all the previous ones. It warrants a systems review, some sort of calibration, and a recommendation to address the errors before they become more of a major issue.

There is a dangerous and complacent acceptance that allows the error to remain in place, when those in power are silent around the reality that the original system was set up to keep targeted groups of the population from making decisions for themselves. I recognize that the candidate and the party who benefited from the irregular outcomes would not want a review, a change in the process, or a correction for the exceptions (small and large) so that outcomes fall within a standard. It is alarming that the party which has never benefited from this antiquated system appears quite complacent in their repeated losses. Thermometers, machines, centrifuges, automobile performance and emissions, even reagent reactions have a standard range of performance acceptability before they need repair, calibration, or discard for persistent malfunctioning. What will it take for the electoral system to reach a similar standard of operation?

The Candidate and Leadership Practice

Speaking of systems calibration, women experience significant struggle and personal cost to get to the senior executive level.[8] Some of the pervasive barriers in place that contribute to the underrepresentation of women in the executive or chief level positions of companies and nations were evident in this public interview. The essential aspects of leadership culture that need to be reshaped to develop and sustain the next generation of women leaders were visible to the discerning eye. Key aspects in relation to workplace occurrences included:

1. There would be no wage gap in this position. The standard salary would apply for any candidate who was in the top position. An interesting lesson that corporations would do well to emulate.

2. The leadership gap still remains. There continues to be considerable barriers for female candidates when it comes to top leadership positions.[8]

3. The selection process or competition was too protracted, continuing even after it was clear the candidate had won the primary and or had earned the party nomination. From my perspective this situation caused Clinton, to be further damaged from ammunition provided to the opposing party going into the general election that was not necessary. Sanders refused to cede the win to Clinton who had undeniably won the victory,

contentiously holding out as the nomination was not yet formally conferred, rather than coming together to strengthen the party position around the common goals. In essence, the female candidate was fighting on all fronts (inside and outside) and continued to have to fight long after she should have been able to pivot to unify the party or to prepare for the general election. Women are socialized and it is expected for them to play nice. In her previous loss, she worked hard to unify the party it seemed behind Obama. Sanders, however, was not so inclined on her behalf. I have wondered whether it was because Sanders was not truly a democrat and could not consider losing to a woman? Or whether it was because she was a female candidate and not accepted as leader? The internal challenge also appeared to be focused on her message.

4. The focus on her message incorporated a significant attempt to dilute, reshape or alter the focus of Clinton's message and what would be the party platform. It appeared that Sanders additionally held out for them to incorporate or adopt more of his positions as contingency for his conceding what he had already lost. He was partially successful in muddying the waters and the message.

5. The message however, remained clear enough for Clinton to 1) win the popular vote by 2.8+ million votes. Beyond that, 2) the message continues to be followed today. Ironically, the 'Stronger Together'[9] slogan is now a necessary way of life for large segments of the population, and a means for national survival. The slogan became a method for safeguarding followers' voices when as silence-breakers they took back their personal power, and a way to ensure leadership accountability for the American people.

6. The 'good old boys club' could also have been in operation as it closed ranks against her nomination resulting in being placed in the top position in the nation. Each did their part independently but with cumulative net effect. The club members would consist of Sanders as indicated in points 2 and 3. Trump the other party opponent. Comey the one who broke campaign convention and brought out new information about Clinton emails just a few days before the election, effectively railroading the campaign. Then there was Putin, who lent his assistance indirectly in the process of achieving his goal. Then there were the committees that spent years and millions of dollars in relentless but fruitless investigations which left an indelible mark on her life in the public eye. Her years of service to the public and country were marred by a prevailing mistruths and perceptions of being untrustworthy, not likable, and inauthentic.

7. After the loss which had to have been both shocking and quite painful, Clinton took time for self-reflection. Time to assess, heal, destress and regroup all would have been necessary. One level involved the candidate's self-silencing. However, there was also another level of public silencing at play where it seemed that as a public we did not want to face or truly discuss what had actually happened to us. The media took their positions and their packaged talking points, called for her to be silent and even disappear were that possible. It was odd, that as they processed what had occurred, followers appeared frustrated and as if they just wanted to erase the candidate from memory as the country grappled with the unprecedented rising number of votes, while pretending that what was occurring was normal. Speaking about erasure, the Texas State Board of Education, voted to erase Clinton out of the history textbooks.[10]

It is important to restate that neither education or leadership is value neutral. Removing the candidate from the history textbooks as a leader is a values-based concerted effort to continue to spread the metanarrative of mistruths, to lie by omission and leave out a critical woman from our history, spinning(or re-writing) a skewed story of our history this is atrocious. By keeping the candidate out of the history books distorts the truth of what actually occurred and maintains the myth that women cannot lead. The final aspect of silencing was a sad reality that many people get their opportunity to make the circuit to promote and sell their book, Clinton's tour was called a 'whine tour' as if as the person (or embodiment) of the experience she was not allowed to explain or discuss her side of reality though others could discuss it.

Dismissed as a 'not a good candidate' or 'loser,' it took some time for the enormity of the system's brokenness to be seen and acknowledged, but it was discussed as if the broken system was uncritically acceptable. The broken electoral college system is sporadically talked about as the next election nears, but those who hold power because of it will not move for fear of jeopardizing their chances of staying in power by fixing it. It has not yet been dealt with to date. I believe this is also the corporate modus operandi when it comes to women. Broken or inequitable selection systems, women's underrepresentation, the wage gap, exclusion from strategic networks, the narratives and the silencing are sustained and perpetuated because to change it jeopardizes leader's perceived chances of staying in power if women were given equal access to top leadership positions. The silencing is also part of the corporate system as described in an earlier chapter as well. Companies do the same thing to women in similar situations, hoping that by silencing them they will go way.

Silencing the Individual

From my perspective, it can be that the pain and aftermath of these struggles leaves the leader temporarily silenced (reflective; assessive; self-regulatory; restorative) in the immediate aftermath to gain time to process and articulate what had truly happened to person as a woman and as a leader. In the organization this can include things like being led to believe and feeling betrayed by those who you thought would advocate for or sponsor you, coming to terms with an organizational psychological contract that had been broken, or having to smile and keep on working alongside the person who was promoted to the position that was denied you. It can also mean that while the organization is willing to 'pick your brain' for the solution they so desperately seek, they may also be unwilling to place you, the woman, in the position where the value of such knowledge creation is required daily for the organization's benefit and rewarded. Such acknowledgement would also require formal recognition of the capability and competency of the woman and that still continues to be a problem. This signals that organizations are not yet ready for, or amenable to, the demands of required change.

Gender and Amenability to Women's Leadership

Another intriguing phenomenon was that women suddenly became galvanized and up in arms. Beginning the day after the election, women began signing up in unprecedented numbers to run for office. The first wave of the sea -change occurred the day after the inauguration when about half a million women marched on Washington and around the nation. The second wave occurred in the 2018 election when the House of Representatives[11] saw its largest and most diverse class of female freshmen, intentional about taking over leadership by becoming leaders themselves locally and nationally. This is the definition of revolution in its first form I presented. The power of cultural socialization as outlined in chapter one as the underpinning of decision heuristic is unquestionable. I have frequently wondered about and reflected on how we ended up where we did as a country. The obvious answer could be that Clinton was a woman and the country would take any male over a woman in keeping with the status quo. However, here, from a cultural perspective, the decisions made in this context can also speak to the whole issue of timing. Sometimes the timing is not right. Perhaps Clinton was ahead or on the early point of the country's maturity curve. Yes, even after 242 years of existence, but if she had not engaged the race so persistently, change would not have become a point of consideration. It could be that all things were not in alignment and as an aspirant women are told it is important to have personal patience (for the opportunity that does not come) or you may need to leave that particular company for a company that seeks out women's talent because it is valued. Easier said than done for a country.

In conversations about women and leadership the social ethos and priorities for change, (which has ethical underpinnings for decision-making) have been race, then gender. Civil Rights before women's rights. still working on the equal pay. the country's zeitgeist, as in readiness for change and advancement, is one that followed this order for selecting the country's top leader as well. Race in the form of a President Obama, a black male, also a historical first, came before gender in the possibility of a Clinton historical first-woman presidential party nomination. Yet, the prevailing mood remains non-readiness for women's top leadership. Conflict in part is a knowledge that change was needed, coupled with the desire for the change not to be embodied in a woman. Change would demand a grappling and coming to terms with whether the revolutionary presence of the first woman as commander in chief could be the one that the country can live with.

Culture and Leadership Decision Making

The force of culture or perception on our collective decision-making was evident in our society's decision along the lines of gender in 2008, and again in 2016. I am optimistic to note that there is an expectation, even a demand for a woman to be on the ticket in the 2020 race and hoping that we will be more willing to vote for her at this point in time. The second definition of revolution presented, involves a seismic social sea-change in the way leadership is perceived with potential ripple effect across society, organizations in both the public and private spheres. The public was ready, but leaders and the system were not ready. I believe that when the system fails the very people it was designed to help it needs to be changed or rethought. For women it means being granted their equal rights or ratifying Amendment 28, something that still needs to be completed. It also means being granted access to top leadership positions in a context that is more inclusive and accepting of their leadership competencies. Was gender an issue? Was the faulty system which does not work to enfranchise every voter? Perhaps, because voters *for* Clinton as woman candidate ran up the score. Some quickly push the truth about this unexamined situation on the backburner of silence to avoid needed change. You can draw your own conclusions.

Though other candidates claimed a revolution or that they started a movement, the real revolution and change in the fundamental fabric of society (politics, leadership, gender role perception, and a woman's ability to transcend barriers) was embodied by Clinton's historic candidacy for president of the United States. The voters' election of Clinton would have fit the definition of a revolution, and would have been a "direct repudiation and the thorough replacement of an established government or political system by the people governed"[4] The historic possibility of a President Hillary Clinton (or the woman that becomes the first president) would have indeed been "a radical and pervasive change in society and the social structure"[4] in a way that none of the other candidates could ever approximate in a positive way. The quest? To make it a more inclusive republic. The physical embodiment of national leadership in a woman, as something that the United States has never seen before fundamentally would have shifted the prevailing paradigms of male leadership that has predominated for 240 years -that would be radical. This movement would have signaled an openness and embrace of new leadership possibilities for the nation, its society, sectors and businesses in a way that was unprecedented. Openness to women's leadership at this level would initiate change in the social structure by the governed, and would fundamentally shift the political system.

Revolutionary Violence and Violence in Women's Leadership

The final component of the definition of a revolution is that often times it is accompanied by strong resistance and violence. Even the campaign rhetoric increasingly leaned toward an explicit openness to violence and misogyny: calls to lock up the opponent candidate, threats to lock her up if she wins, or explicit calls for violent reaction to the outcome of the election, which can accompany any revolution in terms of a mounted resistance to change. One could argue that this is a sudden occurrence if there has not been especial attention paid to the shifting dynamics of women taking on leadership positions -in society, politics, organizations and around the world. I connect this back to the violence and threat that is inherent in a leader's exercise of power and control, and the coercive methods some will employ to get there. This raises the very real specter of physical, sexual, and psychological violence which is no longer beneath the surface of civility.

The Fight for the Comfort of the Status Quo

The part significant to our discourse on the treatment of women as leaders and an indication of the public's generalized feelings on women are the liberal use of the 'B-word,' the vitriolic sexually abusive slogans on T-shirts, a reality that women still will refuse to support each other collectively, instead aligning with males who control a power system or leadership culture oppressive to them. It is the name-calling that is destructive of one's character and reputation, or that the media in their quest for objectivity and providing information repeats or replays the negativity over and over until it becomes something of a mantra, though there may be no truth or evidence to it. It seems we are collectively dismissive of the disrespect of women or not even aware of it when it shows up in words, behaviors or actions of people. It is as if women are not equally deserving of the respect of humanity, or what they have earned as part of their track record. In addition, the track record though it may be impressive, is dismissed as inconsequential when compared to that of a less qualified male, and in fact, it is frequently turned into a negative perception of being power hungry or overly ambitious for women though the same impressive accomplishments are praised and even encouraged in men who already have power and don't hide their ambition.

Power Differentials and Whose Voice we Hear

It continues to be frustrating and challenging that when women speak in tones of authority, raise their voice, or sounds angry, one of the immediate responses is to say they are hysterical, screaming or if they are black they are 'angry black women'. Alternatively, the response is that the woman is not clear about what she said or meant. The raised voices can come from other men, but not from women. Well, the anger emotion is not exclusive to men, though society has virtually made it so by taking away the other emotions (such as sadness or tears). Another response is to ignore women or to act as if they haven't spoken at all. In this case it should be noted that the candidate's voice was modulated, measured and competent. The narrative surrounding the candidate's slogan 'stronger together,' is still repeatedly ridiculed by analysts and commentators as not being a 'clear message.' Yet, the message was patently clear, adopted and embodied by the millions of women who marched in protest movements and rallies. Unity is the only way that fundamental change will happen in the fabric of this country's culture. Clinton's competence undeniable. I believe it scared leaders, men and women alike -globally. Yet, as often happens in companies, she was passed over. Unless our paradigms change, the patriarchal society will continue to embrace the power differential that accepts the voice of men raised in authority over women's voices. Women's voices when asserted will continue to be criticized or ignored, unless they are amplified until normalized, because of the power differential given to men in a patriarchal society. How then do we address the revolution which has begun as a result of the woman candidate?

Ultimately, the 2016 election experience could be illustrated by a fork in the road with the country having to choose which road they would like to travel for the next four years. I believe that the unexplainable unfounded gender-based aversion to the female candidate was driven by the false narratives built over the years about Clinton, by implicit gender biases fostered by a societal culture in which women are still not considered to be equal. There continue to be men and women who still cannot countenance the reality and benefit of a woman leading them. As a result, the last few lines of Robert Frost's poem *The Road Not Taken*[12] aptly exemplify the electoral college's decision. In this context, the lines of the final verse would read:

I shall be telling this with a sigh

Somewhere ages and ages hence:

Two roads diverged in a wood, and we-

We took the one *most* traveled by,

And that has made all the difference.

The existential fear, anxiety, anger, and frustration of the people who felt they were no longer important in an economy where technology had made their skills obsolete. people fear impending mindset shift of adopting new skills, connected with the ideals and the rhetoric of both male candidates, in an antiquated system not calibrated for the increasing margin of error called disenfranchisement. It ultimately culminated in a loss for the female candidate, though she really won. America refused the road less traveled by, and it has certainly made a significant difference. So, what leadership lessons can we learn from this experience?

In leadership practice I've observed that many still cannot envision the benefits of having a female leader in the highest position in the nation, and of the free world, as is often said in the same breath. The false metanarrative about women's capacity (or lack of it) to lead remains a question in the minds of men and women alike. Women's leadership threatens the power differentials fundamentally necessary for a sexist patriarchal system to operate.[13] The resistance to making necessary changes in prevailing mental models remains one of the major action steps many companies still need to take. The myths and spins played out in front of our eyes. For instance, the myth of women's weakness, leadership competency and physical endurance were demonstrated when as Secretary of State Clinton endured 11 hours of interrogation and remained even-tempered, cogent and even demonstrated a sense of humor to the chagrin of the congressional panel who ultimately could not find anything. Strength was demonstrated in one of the debates when attempts were made by the opposing candidate and women who sought to publicly humiliate and shame with her husband's infidelity. A focused and balanced emotional management and self-regulation were personal power on display. Other evidence of calmness and self-control and competent ability was demonstrated when her personal space and professional boundaries were invaded as she was stalked while she was answering a question from the audience. In this instance was demonstrated how many women have to continue leading in abusive cultures in the workplace. Few observers did not recognize what was going on. Anecdotally from conversations, it was quite viscerally threatening to some female onlookers. I personally wondered why the moderators did not weigh in, or why the media did not make the connection to abusive behavior of women in society and the workplace. As often happens, the assessment was not based on her competence, it was based on whether she would fall apart or not. A 'test' that men are not subjected to. It was personal power on display to keep her focus on providing the answer while recognizing the breach of personal and professional boundaries. The reality? Subsequent to enduring such a public societally sanctioned and enabled emotional and psychological abuse, in front of millions of viewers, rather than falling apart as intended, the candidate's ability to maintain composure and keep her wits about her to answer audience questions or to present policy positions cogently is the hallmark of a strong and competent leader. It debunks the myth of women's weakness. The phenomenal courage and inner strength that it took to publicly face down that kind of psychological and emotional abusive behavior, while the world looked on, as the first female major party nominee in the country's existence, demonstrates a level character, fortitude, and resilience is rare – still yet before its time, and perhaps not yet understood or respected for its exceptionality, and ultimate benefit for the country as a whole.

However, this demonstration of mental strength, physical stamina, memory, and agile intellect with incisive clarity was held against her: using the spin of her not being emotional (human) or not smiling enough. I daresay that had the candidate shown an emotional reaction; media and the public would have gladly thrown it back at her by calling her too emotional, or the favorite word of the spin in this instance is 'hysterical.' A feat few individuals could accomplish while maintaining a calm and steady demeanor. The candidate's political opponent actively continued to perpetuate the spin of women's weakness throughout the campaign.

Leadership culture. In the candidacy of the first female major party nominee in a developed country we looked into a two-way mirror of contemporary workplace leadership culture in the following ways. We saw on public display, at the national level with millions of viewers, some of the abusive behaviors that America's women are subjected to in the workplace and in society daily. It became a visceral and deeply uncomfortable vicarious stalking experience for many observing women. As an observer, there was a feeling and memory of unease, anxiety and threat, fear, a sense of déjà-vu. Women unwittingly witnessed how women could be physically threatened and bullied by abusive men -or leaders. As a woman and leader, I wanted her to at minimum reclaim her space. At maximum to challenge him, confront or call him out in relation to what he was doing to the whole world. It was a study in abusive leadership behavior between leader-colleagues, an illustration of how many women are or can be silenced in the presence of transgression intimidating behavior in the hope of achieving a professional goal. Keeping her cool, producing high performance, while the threat is tangibly and physically present. The incident also highlights how threatening and abusive behavior can get cursory mention in the media, vigorous defensive rationalization and dismissal as just being alpha male by male onlookers, and insufficient resistance from those who knew it to be wrong. We witnessed a layered traumatic and violent experience which was personal and painfully humiliating as it also involved the woman candidate being shamed for her husband's past transgression behavior.

What was also witnessed, and contributed to, was the lack of accountability or consequence that is still patently prevalent in leadership practice today. It is the connection between leadership and violence against women. Where individuals who have a history of violence against women continue to be promoted, rewarded and granted positions of authority over followers uncritically to those who display abusive behavior -such as the office of the presidency or CEO of a company. It was striking to note that many of the analysts of this behavior were men, who were not unified in their condemnation of such behavior. The women analysts could not all clearly articulate what they saw, and some women participated in the humiliation exercise This also happens in corporations. It is my position that more men need to break the code of silence, and speak up about abusive behavior, alongside women who will resist engaging in the abuse and humiliation of another woman to hold the perpetrators accountable by not condoning, protecting or rewarding such behavior. We can no longer remain silent bystanders or those who do not want to get involved. It is time to be engaged the effect is closer to you than you think.

Sexism to make her look ineffectual, misogyny, the doctored videos, trying to make her look weak. Because she is actually strong others are afraid of what she brings to the table. The decorum is lost, the lowest tactics employed, and it is as if the culture relishes the takedown and embarrassment of the woman leader in question. The challenge is the critical thinking ability of the viewers, the lack of accountability by technology platforms to take them down. Yet, many voters saw through the ruse. The stalking, the taking up of her personal space or her 'real-estate' as if she had no right or entitlement to being -and winning- on the same stage he was on. It was designed to rattle her (she remained calm), it was designed to cause her to lose her train of thought (she stayed the course of keen clarity). The other issue is her being punished for her husband's transgression (a pattern that is replayed with blaming the victim for perpetrator transgressions.

It must be quite difficult to live with the ironically painful paradox of having won yet having lost. It also must be equally painful and galling to know that the record will forever shows you didn't truly win, but the win was still given to you because of the system. In terms of the double standard, the bar remains low for men, unreasonably high for women. Then when women scale it, they are blamed for doing so. The irrefutable question of what might have been had we taken the road less travelled by haunts me, and I suspect it haunts both candidates on a daily basis. The jury is still out on whether we can learn from our decision, but our choices make all the difference.

Leadership Implications and Conclusions

A return to the way things used to be rather than being the change that is going to be needed, could be as Solomon, the wisest man on earth, put it 'like a dog returning to its vomit' (Proverbs 26: 11; 2 Peter 2:22, NIV). For the leadership and work worlds it would be 1) the unethical lack of foresight that Greenleaf[14] talks about, where leaders see patterns of underrepresentation, or unequal pay and ignore them for the status quo; or, in light of the statistical evidence that women in leadership improve the bottom line and company competitiveness, and not placing them in leadership because men have always led is another.

At the societal level, it is knowing that we are a nation of immigrants yet want to return to a time when forced immigration and overt discrimination were the routine evil of the day despite the equal opportunity laws of the Land. It also means that we are willing to return to a sordid past where slavery and white supremacy were the order of the day, even though we know it is a past that is so painfully shameful that we still cannot talk about it today. America's guilt of the past is the hypocrisy of sending hundreds of thousands overseas to fight a war over the genocide of one race, while perpetrating the same thing on another race at home. It also means that there are still prevalent false perception that things were better then, and that there is a desire to be in a world where liberty, justice, and privilege are for some and not for all. It's a world where power and money, which are neither good nor evil has been into unethical crimes due to uncommon greed. It is a world where globalization though it is here to stay, would be ignored, and the knowledge that we need to change (new skills and competencies) to live in this world that includes trading for resources and services that other countries have, and recognition that in an interconnected global ecosystem we cannot produce or use everything by ourselves. As a nation some of these concepts have been verbally, societally and legally been rejected, yet, somehow they are always on the voters' ballots as we make the decision whether to hold on to the past traditional forms of leadership, or to embrace the future with new forms of leadership. Current systems are weakened, some are defunct. The country cannot continue on this path and remain viable into the future for generations to come. It will require leadership that leads the people to the America of the future. Is it because the change that we seek and need may be personified in the leadership of a woman that it is so vehemently rejected? This becomes all the more reason for women to feel encouraged and empowered to honor their hard-wire to lead. The world and our country desperately need you.

Precís

Women are largely left in leadership practice with having to prove their capability to lead, without having opportunities to lead. The benefit of role models who have successfully learned to navigate the organizational environment and scale the hurdles presented to them is also lacking. Proposed changes that will be required need to occur at several levels in the organization, and even across society, for it to be truly effective, meaning that learning and change also needs to occur. This case study illustrated the experiences of a woman pioneer who went through a public selection process for the top CEO of the nation. She was called to lead when the system and leadership practice in the nation were not ready for her. Contemporary organizations show similar behaviors behind closed doors. Our country and our corporations must find ways to effectively and strategically take into consideration the complexity of the leadership culture for female candidates without jettisoning all of the problems at her feet, then silencing, blaming and rationalizing away her orchestrated failures. Women have responded in a revolutionary way by taking back their power in waves. The system must course correct and become inclusive in order to remain viable and sustainable.

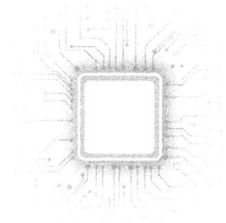

CHAPTER 14

Honoring Your Hard-Wire

*"To be yourself in a world that is constantly trying to make you something else is the greatest accomplishment"_*Ralph Waldo Emerson.

The leadership hard-wire is programmed internally and made stronger or weaker in certain environments, though never fully erased. The environment either fosters and nurtures the individual's predisposition to lead or hinders and negates it. For some women this determines the outcome of their careers. Other women leave the workplace to become their own CEO's because they find that the script, mold or box that corporate, academic or service entities seeks to force them into does not fit. These women change the context to suit their requirements. As women, they are respected but not always celebrated for their difference. Their unique genius is frequently dismissed, rejected, disrespected and devalued as having too much ambition, too high aspirations, or thinking too big.

Yet, in spite of this, the state of women-owned businesses report provides two key points that are encouraging. First, that "as of 2014, there are nearly 9.1 million women-owned enterprises, employing nearly 7.9 million workers and generating over $1.4 trillion in revenues."[1] Second, that in 2019, the number of women-owned firms grew at a rate of 2½ times the national average. And revenue and employment growth among women-owned firms tops that of all other firms—except the largest, publicly traded corporations."[1,2] Women who are hard-wired to lead are finding alternative paths to honoring and expressing their leadership when the contemporary organization culture does not provide a context that includes them. Rather than allowing others to define them, neutralize their light, or scramble the hard-wire, women are taking the initiative to honor their leadership hard-wire as entrepreneurs. While entrepreneurship could be said to be the more difficult alternative route, in the last two decades, the number of women-owned businesses grew 114% with firms owned by women of color grew at a rate of 467%.[2,3] This indicates that women can and do lead and are doing so in unprecedented ways.

Hard-wire and the Code of Silence

Women's hard-wire to lead in contemporary society, as far as we have come, still remains in danger of being infected with viruses and malware or re-wired to suit the social scripts for image, gender, sex, money, church, and ethics in leadership. While the experiences described may not be the experience of all women, far too many women still have them. It is also crucial to be able to support them as their experiences are shared. Knowing about the experiences described in this and the previous volumes prepares the reader to recognize these behaviors and practices when they are encountered. So, this *Hard-Wired to Lead Series* was intended to get the good news to women that you can honor your hard-wire to lead. No matter what the circumstances or the workplace and society try to tell you, there's no need to be imprisoned in the conflicts generated by limited social scripts of gender, race, and privilege, even if there are very few role models available.[3] The intentionally generated challenges are designed to silence and limit your social and upward mobility. There is personal freedom and empowerment in self-definition, in defining your image based on your hard-wire, and knowing your intrinsic worth based on the value you bring to the organization and the world. The discussion on the various power secrets was presented to open the eyes or assist with the recovery of sight for those whose eyes have been blinded by peculiar effect that persistent false narratives can have on the perception of any group in society. If the false narratives are told long enough, systematized, normalized and reinforced in leadership practice, then the truth of women's true capacity and leadership capability will continue to be mischaracterized to fit the mental models that cloud the ability of onlookers to clearly see what women bring to the table. The fact is that women can lead and have been shown to do so effectively when given the opportunity. I hoped that uncovering the power secrets and breaking the code of silence would be helpful in moving toward collaboratively changing prevailing mental models. The goal in the final volume is to present an inclusive reconstructed leadership practice that facilitates the shift to a new leadership culture of the 21st century and beyond. Women are educated, experienced, competent and empowered. Will companies be ready to receive them or still be mired in the myopia of limiting mental models that hamper their company's health, growth and profits?

What does this reconstructed leadership look like? It is one where women can lead unapologetically, where companies can benefit from the creativity and profit brought to the company from the genius inherent in women's connected, collaborative leadership. A leadership culture where truth is based on talent, competence and evidence of effectiveness, not on shades of truth designed to keep women out of leadership positions. Rather, leadership must be inclusive enough to empower the spirit of resilience and encourage women to break the silence to have the open and honest conversations with self and others around their hard-wire, passion, and aspirations. These important dialogs will enhance ability to communicate the critical need for acceptable professional non-abusive conduct in the workplace. Courage will be required for leaders and women to conduct and act on these conversations not only in terms of behavior, but also in terms of fair and equitable negotiated value for women's contributions to company viability. These conversations will also clarify for women whether they can remain in the company or whether they will be better off with movement toward personal expansion to entrepreneurship. Women at this stage are self-determining, authentic, with healthy belief systems and confident in their personal power enough to be true to their leadership hard-wire. Here's what this can look like.

The Fifth Hard-Wired Image and Healthy Belief Systems

A new image of resistance to the status quo is created by women who are hard-wired to lead. The Hard-wire controls the image guiding it towards leadership. However, it is the woman's unique make-up that controls how it is manifested, which makes room for images that are unique, flexible and adaptable to who she is, the system in which she chooses to work or has opportunity to lead, the relationships and the lifestyle she chooses to have, all of which also hold true to the self she has become. It is an integrated image that may result in emotional labor for this authentic woman. One such example of embodied leadership can be found in the former First Lady of the United States, Michelle Obama. Beloved by many, she walked in the power of integrated authentic leadership, projected strategic conceptual visioning as a wise strong, educationally and professionally prepared leader. Her power and influence, as she led by example, was evidenced in her ability to change a fashion designer's or retailer's fame and fortune overnight, with a single dress or outfit that she wore. It was widely known that others would want to follow her choices and lead. I believe that the values she stood for and lived were also attractive to many. Mrs. Obama represented the everyday woman who had made it to the top, fulfilling the American Dream. But she also tapped into a level of leadership authenticity and unique style which integrated a warm, personable, and insightful person which was refreshing. Yet, there were photo-shopped parodied pictures by those who wished to portray her in a negative light.

The leadership image she personified, and her personal power were well outside of the limited acceptable societal (controlling) image or box designated for women of color. This was unsettling to some people. Her power was also evident with her capacity shift a national cultural approach to healthy eating choices, practices and standards with her personal engagement and example. Yet, there were the persistent attempts by some to portray her as non-feminine and I was reminded of the controlling images I addressed in the first volume. Here's what I mean. In terms of integrating Collins' prevailing images, discussed in Volume 1, traces of the images were evident at different times for different reasons. For example, the ethic of care was not missing. It was evident in her caretaker and nurturing image utilized as first lady, to focus on nurturing the health of her own children, the nation's children, and girls' global educational needs world-wide. Aspects of the matriarch were present as the family's needs were skillfully managed, along with public interactions and scrutiny because of the office her husband held. Ironically, though she would not have been dependent on the welfare state outside of this position, nonetheless, the family was dependent on the state for income, their housing and their protection because of their leadership position. Other contemporary and known Fifth Image examples include the case study candidate Hillary Clinton, Nancy Pelosi, Theresa May, Angela Merkel, Susan Rice, Oprah Winfrey, Serena Williams, and Loretta Lynch. Yes, the list is growing for women of color as well and there are many more and we need to know about and highlight them as models of the fifth image, each coming with their own unique cost. This is just a short list of women of power, and I present others as examples throughout this work. The point is to highlight their willingness to follow their hard-wire to lead, be the pioneers willing to blaze trails where there are none, deal with presented challenges and show what can be possible with empowered self-determination. Each is a pioneer example for other women to study and follow as examples of how a hard-wire to lead can uniquely manifest itself in women of power. The numbers may be few, but they are rapidly growing and there is room for many more, including you.

The women of the self-defined fifth image can wear hair natural, straight, in locks or braids, or any way they please; they lead in government as public servants, head businesses or own them and make their way to prominence in their communities and cultures because of their unique genius skill and competence. For those still trying to forge their formidable image though shaped by the myriad experiences embodied, take heart. You may have done everything that society has said needs to be done for advancement, yet still find yourself in poverty, upside down financially, blamed for your own lack of advancement, and ashamed that the formula does not work for you. Well create your own formula. Blaze your own path. It has worked for the 'firsts' examples, the four percent of CEO's and we would see the opportunities expanded to the 96%, or at least to 30% by 2030. Well-educated, well-prepared and presented with lucrative opportunities they move up in the ranks, they lean into opportunities that become available and are financially rewarded for their efforts for the most part. The same level of strength and consummate self-confidence of the fifth image will be required; as well as the authenticity to be who you are, and be able to speak truth to power (wisely, strategically, authentically) but have the courage to make your move if your best prospects are not where you are at present. It is also the recognition that the loss of one opportunity, always opens up other possibilities.

Healthy Belief Systems and New Mental Models

As women, and as leaders, if we have bought into any part of the shades of truth, the convenient self-serving 'blindness' of privilege then our own belief systems and mental models need to be addressed as part of the change in leadership culture. It was clear that the effect of faulty mental models, supported by stories over time serve to shape the actions and behaviors of actors on both sides of the equation. Williamson captures the mindset that can ensue from hegemony (leadership or dominance of one social group over another) and socialization (adapting behavior to the norms or culture of society) in the first part of her statement:

Our deepest fear is that we are powerful beyond measure. It is our light, not our darkness that most frightens us. We ask ourselves, Who am I to be brilliant, gorgeous, talented, fabulous? Actually, who are you *not* to be? You are a child of God. Your playing small does not serve the world.[4]

The quote speaks to the perceived radical nature of women who follow hard-wired to lead. Women who embrace their leadership nature and the qualities that they possess in totality, and ask why not? Why can't I? These women have moved past feeling bad because they out-perform others. In fact, significant out performance has, and will continue to be required for consideration and for the competition of entrepreneurship. Women will no longer feel the need to dumb-down to make others feel comfortable in their presence or to fit in a leadership culture that made little room for them. Rather it is about collaborating and leading the learning structures that need to be in place in the organization to see the transformation in 21st century leadership culture. And, yes, women may have to lead here too. Women do not want to fit in men's shoes. They were not intended to. Instead, the vision is for a leadership world where women's and men's shoes are equally valued and welcomed regardless of size. A place of transformed and reconstructed bias-free leadership practice where women can bring their shoes and be welcomed, their presence and leadership normalized, valued and expected. Women no longer want to be in the 'old boys club' but in the 'leaders club' where the presence of women will have become a best practice standard, with a culture of collaboration and learning that produces systems and organization sustainability.

The personal reality is that if one is hard-wired to lead, it can be quite risky -especially in the beginning. Leading women never really fit in anyway and as women leaders you must be ok with that knowledge, and courageously willing to take the risk. The first female presidential nominee's putting herself in the race is a testament to having come to terms with the risk of seeking the highest office in the land, the risk inherent in stepping up to making of history, demonstrating the painful, sometimes crushing difficulty of charting a course that has not existed before, and going further than others have gone before. The stark reality is that no matter what you do even your authenticity can be misrecognized and dismissed. Some will even seek to write you out of the history books -as if the contributions of your race, gender, hard work, trailblazing, and phenomenal accomplishments never existed.[4] It is so much easier to look better if the other person is silenced. But the value of spiritual stability and healing reflection are critical here in support of the courage and the resilience that are needed to honor that hard-wire and to keep coming back from set back after set back, to make a final comeback. That is if timing permits it. But the hard-wire does not allow some women to play small. Knowing that what you bring to the table is more than enough. Your gift of leadership is designed to serve others and is sorely needed regardless of what others might choose to say. Women are not absolved from using their voices and gifts to create a better world, even in the face of opposition. But beyond that, recognize that by earning and stepping into that leadership position you embody the hope of other aspiring women -young and old- of envisioning the possibility of having potential for leadership experiences because they witnessed someone else's journey. At the societal level, it assuages the heart of older women who fought in suffrage, who were or are trailblazers in their own way, and propels the next generation of women leaders if they are willing to learn from the trailblazers before them.

A Few Last Comments for Women Who are hard-wired to lead

I began this volume with this thought: if you are hard-wired to lead it is *in* you and will be related to your destiny and purpose whether society, company, or family agree with it or not. Marian Wright Edelman states

"No one has the right to rain on your dreams." Therefore, even if you have explained it away, covered it up because of the rain of others, or tried to squeeze it into a box that pleases others, the dream embodied hardwire will be relentlessly seeking an outlet for its fulfilled existence. The issues for women of color are more acute, more consequential because of our collective, yet unresolved history. Yet, we cannot truly progress as a nation or see the needed corporate changes until the perceived 'least of these' have been taken care of. Thus, when we take care of the issues of women of color, the issues of other disenfranchised groups are also addressed under that umbrella. A case in point is the Civil Rights Act originated to help Black people and amended to take care of the rights of other marginalized groups. There is the face of a woman of color on the cover of this volume. Why? Because of the affirmative action borne out of the civil right movement benefited white women primarily. In leadership the persistent 4 of the 5% in top leadership positions is held by white women, and black women hold just at 1%, with minimal Board representation, and the single black female fortune 500 CEO has now retired.[7] Over this reality we are largely silent. A black woman's strongest enemy can be her white sister. I mentioned the Queen Bee phenomenon but remember with the structural context and numerical data is stacked against women of color who are well prepared and well-represented in the aspirant pool. This means that there are also white female executives who will withhold access to leadership opportunity from black female aspirants as well. Over this we are also silent as we pretend to work well together. I have nothing against my white sisters, but they appear to be more interested in the securing the power, privilege and control that safeguards their positional and strategic benefits at the expense of their black counterparts, who are expected to wait for an unspecified appropriate, but unknown time for access to leadership positions they are hard-wired to fill. The narratives and mistruths are designed not only to perpetuate the misrecognition of women of color and their leadership capacity and competency but to scramble the women's hard-wire through manipulation in the process. So that her self-confidence is lost, self-doubt and stress is increased from gaslighting and emotional abuse. Emotional labor is increased with the constant emotional assault and sometimes women personal hard-wired design and purpose is abandoned because the price is too high, or they have been convinced that something is wrong with their wanting to follow the ambitions demanded by their integral design. So, the choice women then have is to keep fighting your nature or you can unapologetically embrace it, refine it, and allow the light of your joy and passion to shine on others. This book was written to express what women who aspire to leadership positions might have experienced or have seen others endure and not been able to speak about it. Awareness takes the stress away, developing relationships and talking with others will take the sting and stigma away and empowers responsible action in response to what you know. Now is the time to walk in your calling and to express your gift. There will be no better time. However, it will require some critical characteristics that will be very important to walking in your calling. The requirements include resilience, courage, strength, creativity, emotional intelligence and connections.

Resilience Factor

The ability to bounce back after discouragement, setbacks or failures will be vital throughout your life and career. It is well known that leaders need vision, strategy, competence, courage and resilience. But when women lead, more is required! The bar is higher; the cost is greater, the challenges more. So, the ability to bounce back from challenges and set-backs is a general requirement for women until leadership culture changes. Scott points out "The values at your core are inflexible, but flexibility is required at the edges."[8] Here's where the elasticity of self-regulated resilience comes into play.[9] It is the ability to step back from the situation, accurately assess it and determine your response. I believe that the greatest lesson to be learned for women in leadership or who aspire to lead is resilience, which also requires support and collaboration. Women are re-learning, newly learning, and recognizing in sheer numbers that we are indeed stronger together.[10] Though many would not admit it, the female Candidate was right. Contrary to the narrative that the message was not clear, the message has clearly shaped the current movement, and amplified the voices and leadership of women in a way that is unprecedented. The question becomes can the momentum be sustained to move the stalled needle on women's leadership?

Implications for Leadership Culture

The first steps to confronting and resolving the problem of women's under-representation in leadership is to break the code of silence, and to consciously connect women's individual leadership problems to the broader societal problems of gender, race, sexism and inequality. There is an awakening and movement among women right now, the women's March on Washington and communities nation-wide, the critical voices Town Halls, the demand for accountability from leaders to represent us as we have elected them to do -not themselves and their personal agendas. This movement has translated into a blue wave of women propelled by an unprecedented march to the voter's booth. There is more to come. Part of me believes that women chose to mobilize too late, disregarding the opportunity presented to us by the female candidate. Many women chose hegemony over necessity disregarding the writing on the wall by refusing to go for the 'new' or break from tradition to embrace the needed change (it's the trap of those sneaky old mental models). Perhaps the march on Washington would not have been needed and we know things would have been different. The other part of me recognizes that revolutions are started not when people state it, or even know it is needed. Revolutions start when there is critical mass or a watershed moment constructed from the alignment of social awareness, collective consciousness and concerted purposeful action. Revolutions require a connecting the dots of systemic oppression so that a clear full picture emerges when individuals, groups, and people who have been personally affected by oppression, become sufficiently conscious, and are galvanized with passionate collective action to change their situation. So, there is hope. Daily.

One question remains. Will our desire and opportunity align itself when a similar opportunity presents itself again? There is power in numbers, there is power in collective expression of voice but we must get beyond just awareness, and just talk, to coordinated collective action for changing and re-constructing the perceptual role expectations, women's and human rights, sexual reproductive or self-determination decisions and capacity for leadership- collectively, strategically, and purposively. A central truth to the resistance of familiar mental models for men and society may be the fear that women will take over if allowed equal opportunity. This too is a myth. Women want the ability to walk in their own power and not be restricted to make others comfortable. There is enough leadership need in proportion to the leadership talent that exists. Thus, learning and leadership structures and support systems must also address these issues in a collaborative movement toward collective corporate and societal change. For generational learning, leadership must be taught and modeled, and allowed for girls from an early age, so that boys know it is normal and the paradigms are shifted. An unstoppable revolutionary tsunami has begun to disrupt stereotypical and systemic structures that hinder women from fully achieving the leadership and societal culture where women can thrive. I believe those who get on board are wiser and will fare better than those who resist the movement.

Transitioning to an inclusive model of leadership culture is still in progress so in the meantime, contemporary women leaders will need to be integrated, flexible and agile in the workplace with fluidity of movement between the best behavioral characteristics of both men and women. This new form of leadership bridges social role expectations and organizational expectations, while demonstrating competency and effectiveness leadership and remaining true to their gender will become the future norm for sustaining women's leadership. Such leadership is authentic. Not as others would have you to be but purposed and passionately following your hard-wire. The quote at the beginning of the chapter speaks to how society, the workplace and others will seek to change who you are or press you into acting in unethical or contradictory ways which do not align with who you really are. Stay true to your inner Northstar and do not allow others to change your hard-wire and you will never lose your way. Use my R.I.S.E mentoring model: where you Receive mentoring, Impart or mentor others, Share knowledge assertively, and are Empowered to lead.

The needed changes are great and will take sustained and concerted effort on all fronts. Women's collaborative, purposive action can change the socio-cultural environment through their running for office, their vote in the larger social context, for example. It will require the collective exercise of personal power to change the cultural, social, workplace and political leadership culture and context across all levels of society. This would not only be historic, but it has the potential to change the way senior level leadership is perceived across society. In much the same way, for women to proportionately be represented in top executive positions in the public and private corporate world, it will take the collective action of men and women to effect significant leadership culture change inside and outside their organizations with persistent, confident, purposive action. It will require confronting and transcending paradigms, policies and practices that limit women's potential and a shift in leadership culture to one that is more inclusive. The foundational blocks of change, according to Kotter[11] need to be put in place with a sense of urgency. It is the urgency that will propel action at the individual, organizational, and societal levels. Organizations that proactively remove the burden of proof for women will become more strategically viable and effective in the 21st century. Women's knowledge and skills are sorely needed, and the whole world is waiting for them to step into their life's calling. The significance of this is that companies that have women in top positions, or on the governing board, show an increase in innovation, revenue, and decision-making processes. When companies are in the business to make profit and revenue, their collective destinies are irrevocably and directly linked to having women in leading positions if they want to be viable into the 21st century. Educating the workforce is a primary and essential factor in going beyond just raising awareness, to having open dialogue at the decision-making table around the leadership culture of the organization. We tackle this in Volume 3. Coupled with accountability and manager rewards for making the connections between the presence of leading women and increased revenue, and the placement of women in key leadership positions will round out the picture.

The other factors are organizational male supporters, and leader sponsorship, women executives and of course the aspirant candidates. Addressing the issue on all fronts moves beyond the rhetoric and research to action that signals what could well be the cresting next wave of the women's movement, not just for equality of access into the workplace, or equality of compensation, but for women's glass escalator of equal access to the leadership positions they have prepared and worked for but have yet to earn. Such initiatives will result in a fundamental mindset shift in organizational perceptions of women's leadership capability, the legitimization of their leadership, and ultimately the re-shaping of organizational leadership culture to one that is more egalitarian. In so doing, the next generation of women leaders will be strengthened and sustained, and the culture of leadership will have been fundamentally changed to include them well into the future. The world needs and awaits women's leadership and light. So shine, and honor your hard-wire to lead.

Precís

This chapter has summarized key concepts from the book, and provides contemporary examples of the fifth, and proposed hard-wired to lead image for women. It includes a call for women to identify, honor and live out their call to lead. learning structures and support for both men and women, continued open communication and dialogue, and concerted strategic action will ensure that potential is achieved. It also invites the collaboration of leaders, men and women in this quest for equal access to leadership, by changing the mental models that undergird the prevailing leadership culture, so that organizations can also thrive.

Chapter Titles

Volume I – Leadership Context

Title: Hard-Wired to Lead: Power Secrets and Women's Leadership

Poem

Prologue

Chapter 1: When a Leader's Power is Abusive

Chapter 2: The Image Code: Showing Up as Me

Chapter 3: The Gender Code: And I'm A Woman

Chapter 4: The Sex Code: Disrespecting Personal and Professional Boundaries

Chapter 5: The Money Code: She Works Hard for the Money

Chapter 6: The Church Code: Forgive Them, For They Know What They Do

Chapter 7: Code Correction: Retributive and Restorative Justice in the Workplace and in Society

Epilogue: Leadership Context in National Context Why it Matters

Volume III: Leadership ReConstruction

Hard-Wired to Lead: ReConstruction for Women's Leadership

Poem

Prologue

Chapter 15: Ethical Blind Spots and Leader Decision-making

Chapter 16: Learning to Break the Silence: A Radical Approach

Chapter 17: Lead Yourself First: Individual Strategies

BIBLIOGRAPHY

Volume II Prologue

1. Rockefeller Foundation. Women in Leadership: Why it Matters. Global Strategy Group. https://assets.rockefellerfoundation.org/app/uploads/20160512082818/Women-in-Leadership-Why-It-Matters.pdf

2. Sire, J. W. (2009). The universe next door: A basic worldview catalog. 5th ed. Chicago, IL: Intervarsity Press. www.ivpbooks.com.

3. Eagly, A. H & Carli, L. L. (2007). *Through the labyrinth: The truth about how women become leaders.* Boston, MA: Harvard Business School Press.

Chapter 8 Hard-wired: The Leadership Factor

1. Paustian-Underdahl, S. C., Walker , L. S., & Woehl, D. J. (2014, April 28). Gender and perceptions of leadership effectiveness: A meta-analysis of contextual moderators. Journal of Applied Psychology. Advance online publication. 1131-1140 http://dx.doi.org/10.1037/a0036751, pp. 1131-1140

2. McKinsey & Company. (2012). Women Matter: Making the Breakthrough. http://www.mckinsey.com.

3. Senge, P. M. (2006). *The Fifth Discipline: The Art & Practice of the Learning* Organization. New York, NY: Doubleday, a division of Random House, Inc.

4. Nanton, C. R. (2011). Creating leadership legacy: Social learning and leadership development. *International Journal of Learning*, 7(12), 181-193.

5. Northouse, P. G. (2013). *Leadership: Theory and Practice.* Sixth edition. Los Angeles, CA: Sage.

6. Radford, M. H. B. (1996). Culture and its effects on decision making: Crosscultural factors and decision making. In Loke, W. H. (Ed.). *Perspectives on judgment and decision making.* (pp. 49 – 69). Lanham: Scarecrow Press. p. 52

7. Singer, M. H. (1998). Culture: A perceptual approach. In Bennett, M. H. *Basic concepts of intercultural communication: Selected readings.* (pp. 97 – 109). Yarmouth: Intercultural Press. p. 99

8. Nanton, C. R. (2018). The Transfer: Cross-pollinating Violence against women to leadership practice. Boynton Beach: Carmel Connections Inc.

9. www.dictionary.com. Definition of hard-wired.

10. Fels, A. (2004). "Do women lack ambition?" *Harvard Business Review.* On Point. 9424, 2-11.

11. Kehler, K. Quote. https://thoughts-about-god.com/katherine-kehler/nine-leadership-principles

12. AWANA Youth Association (AYA).

13. Bielby, D. D., and Bielby, W. T. (1988, March). She works hard for the money: Household responsibilities and the allocation of work effort. The American Journal of Sociology. Social Science Module. 93(5), 1031 – 1059.

14. O'Hara. M. E. (2017). A Day Without a Woman Draws Protests, Arrests, Around the World. https://www.nbcnews.com/news/us-news/day-without-woman-draws-protests-arrests-around-world-n730651

15. https://www.washingtonpost.com/news/made-by-history/wp/2018/06/18/the-equal-rights-amendment-has-been-dead-for-36-years-why-it-might-be-on-the-verge-of-a-comeback/?noredirect=on&utm_term=.5c912efc0e5d

16. McGregor, J. (2019). In NASA's spacesuit saga women see their own stories. *Washington Post.*

17. Human Factors Engineering. Agency for Healthcare Research and Quality. Patient Safety Primer. US Department of Health and Human Services. https://psnet.ahrq.gov/primers/primer/20

Chapter 9: The Code and Culture of Silence

1. http://www.todayifoundout.com/index.php/2010/11/gun-silencers-dont-make-them-anywhere-near-silent/

2. Catalyst (2012). http://www.catalyst.org/knowledge/women-workforce-united-states#footnote16_7o99cnk

3. dictionary.cambridge.org/dictionary/english/Definition of a code

4. Kibbee, R. (1968) Producer. *It Takes a Thief.* 1968-1970 Television Series

5. Perkins, L. M. (1997). The African American female elite: The early history of African American women in the seven sister colleges, 1880-1960. Harvard Educational Review. 67(4), 718-756. African American families as two-career families, women have always worked outside the home. They could not fulfill the stay at home mother role expectation.

6. VanBooven, V. (2016, May 31). Home Health Care Workers Leaving the Industry Due to Several Factors. HomeCareDaily.com. https://www.homecaredaily.com/2016/05/31/home-health-care-workers-leaving-industry-due-several-factors/ Also, Black women and sexual violence. https://now.org/wp-content/uploads/2018/02/Black-Women-and-Sexual-Violence-6.pdf

Also, NWLC (2018). Black Women Disproportionately Experience Workplace Sexual Harassment, New NWLC Report Reveals. https://nwlc.org/press-releases/black-women-disproportionately-experience-workplace-sexual-harassment-new-nwlc-report-reveals/

7. Schow On Orchestra Wage Dispute: 'This Is Not A Case Of Unequal Pay For Equal Work' Dailywire.com. https://www.dailywire.com/news/schow-orchestra-wage-dispute-not-case-unequal-pay-daily-wire on salary choice instead of gender gap.

8. Willmer, S. (2018, November 19). Goldman Executive dismissed 15 year veteran on maternity leave. Bloomberg. https://www.bloomberg.com/news/articles/2018-11-19/goldman-sachs-star-dismissed-15-year-veteran-on-maternity-leave

9. King, M. L. (1967). Quote. Beyond Vietnam: A time to break Silence, speech delivered on April 4, 1967, at Riverside Church in New York City

10. Nanton, C. R. (2005). Through these gates: African diasporan women's decision to participate in adult education programs. New York, NY: Teachers College Press.

11. Lorde, A. (1983) Sister Outsider: Essays and Speeches. Crossing Press, Feminist Series. The transformation of silence into action. p. 43.

12. hooks, b. (1994). Teaching to Transgress: Education as the practice of freedom. New York: Routledge.

13. Palmer, P. J. (1998). The courage to teach: Exploring the inner landscape of a teacher's life. San Francisco, CA: Jossey Bass Publishers Inc. p. 45

14. Welton, M. (Ed.). (1995). In defense of the lifeworld. Albany, NY: SUNY. Hegemony. p.13…

15. Palmer, N. 2012: The Haves and the "Soon to Haves" Sociology Focus, para 4, retrieved from http://sociologyinfocus.com/tag/hegemony/

16. Freire, P. (1970). *Pedagogy of the Oppressed*. Translated by M. Ramos. New York, NY: Bloomsbury

17. Nanton, C. R. (2018). The Transfer: Cross-pollinating Violence against women to leadership practice. Boynton Beach: Carmel Connections Inc.

18. www.DuluthModel.org.

19. Ellison's (1952/1994). *Invisible Man*. New York, NY: Random Hose.

20. Johnson, C. (1994). Foreword. In Ellison, R. (1947, reprinted 1994. Modern Library Commemorative edition). *Invisible Man*. New York: Random House. (p. vii-viii). ceding

21. Overbeck, J. (2016). Why no self-respecting woman can vote for Hillary. https://townhall.com/columnists/joyoverbeck/2016/10/03/why-no-selfrespecting-woman-can-vote-for-hillary-n2226884; See also https://www.thewrap.com/i-wont-vote-for-hillary-just-because-shes-running-and-female/

22. Drexler, P. (2013, March 6). The Tyranny of the Queen Bee, *Wall Street Journal*.

23. Napikoski, L. (2019, March). Phyllis Schafly and the Stop ERA Campaign. https://www.thoughtco.com/stop-equal-rights-amendment-3528861

24. Anderson, J. (2018). The Estrogen Effect: Huge Study finds that companies with more women leaders are more profitable. *Quartz*. https://qz.com/612086/huge-study-find-that-companies-with-more-women-leaders-are-more-profitable/

25. Richards, and others (1996). Quote on silence divides us in Through These Gates (2005) p.105.

26. Denzin, N. K., & Lincoln, Y. S. (Eds.). (1998). *Strategies of Qualitative Inquiry*. Thousand Oaks, CA: Sage Publications. p. xxi on Silence

27. Goldsmith, E. (1970). *The Ostrich Syndrome*. From a talk given in 1970, para. 26. http://www.edwardgoldsmith.org/717/the-ostrich-syndrome/

Chapter 10: Can Women Lead? The Truth of Women's Leadership Effectiveness

1. Gannon, M. J, and Pillai, R. K . (2013). Understanding global cultures: Metaphorical journeys through 31 nations, clusters of nations, continents, and diversity. Fifth edition. Los Angeles, CA: Sage.

2. Dee Dee Myers Quotes. (n.d.). BrainyQuote.com. Retrieved December 3, 2019, from BrainyQuote.com Web site: https://www.brainyquote.com/quotes/dee_dee_myers_420741

3. Catalyst (2012). http://www.catalyst.org/knowledge/women-workforce-united-states#footnote16_7o99cnk; Data taken from US Census 2011; National Center for Education Statistics, "Table 318.30: Bachelor's, Master's, and Doctor's Degrees Conferred by Postsecondary Institutions, by Sex of Student and Discipline Division: 2013-14" *2015 Digest of Education Statistics* (2015).

4. Perry, M. J. (2017). Women earn majority of doctoral degrees in 2016 for 8th straight year and outnumber men in grad school 135 to 100. http://www.aei.org/publication/women-earned-majority-of-doctoral-degrees-in-2016-for-8th-straight-year-and-outnumber-men-in-grad-school-135-to-100/. www.AEI.org. para. 2.

5. Perry, M. J. (2017). Women earn majority of doctoral degrees in 2016 for 8th straight year and outnumber men in grad school 135 to 100. http://www.aei.org/publication/women-earned-majority-of-doctoral-degrees-in-2016-for-8th-straight-year-and-outnumber-men-in-grad-school-135-to-100/. para 9. Department of Education, NCES 2016-007

6. Warner, J. The women's leadership gap: women's leadership by the numbers. https://www.americanprogress.org/issues/women/reports/2015/08/04/118743/the-womens-leadership-gap/

7. Schow On Orchestra Wage Dispute: 'This Is Not A Case Of Unequal Pay For Equal Work' Dailywire.com. https://www.dailywire.com/

news/schow-orchestra-wage-dispute-not-case-unequal-pay-daily-wire on salary choice instead of gender gap.

8. Nanton, C. R. (2019). *Hard-wired to lead: Power Secrets and Women's Leadership*. Volume 1. Boynton Beach, FL: Carmel Connections Inc. Chapter 5.

9. KPMG Women's leadership Study. Diversity as strategic advantage. https://home.kpmg/content/dam/kpmg/ph/pdf/ThoughtLeadershipPublications/KPMGWomensLeadershipStudy.pdf. See also McKinsey & Company. (2012). Women Matter: Making the Breakthrough. http://www.mckinsey.com.

10. Olsson, S., & Walker, R. (2004) ""Two wo-men and the boys": Patterns of identification and differentiation in senior women executives' representations of career identity." *Women in Management Review*. Women's Interest Module. 19, no. 5/6, 244 –251; Nanton, C. R . & Alfred, M. V. (2009). (Eds.). *Social Capital and Women's Support Systems: Networking, Learning and Surviving*. NDACE I122. San Francisco: Jossey-Bass.

11. Catalyst, 2016 Catalyst Census: Women and Men Board Directors (2017**).** https://www.catalyst.org/research/2016-catalyst-census-women-and-men-board-directors/

12. Christiansen, L., Huidan L., Pereira, J., Topalova, P., Turk R., & Brooks, P. K. (2016). Gender Diversity in Senior Positions and Firm Performance: Evidence from Europe International Monetary Fund.

13. Anderson, J. (2016, February 10) The Estrogen Effect. Huge study finds that companies with more women leaders are more profitable. http://www.executivealliance.org/news/news.asp?id=274186 para.1.

14. Noland, M., & Moran, T. (2016). Study: Firms with more women in the c-suite are more profitable. *Harvard Business Review*. https://hbr.org/2016/02/study-firms-with-more-women-in-the-c-suite-are-more-profitable. para, 2. See also data in Study by https://home.kpmg/

content/dam/kpmg/ph/pdf/ThoughtLeadershipPublications/
KPMGWomensLeadershipStudy.pdf

15. Eagly, A. H., & Johnson, B. T. (1990). Gender and leadership style: A meta-analysis. *Psychological Bulletin*, 108, 233-256. p. 249.

16. DuBrin, A. J. (2007). Leadership: Research Findings, Practice, and Skills. Mason, OH: South Western. p. 125.

17. Hoyt, C. (2013). Women and Leadership. In P. G. Northouse, (2013). Leadership, Theory and

practice. (5th ed).; pp. 349-382. Los Angeles, CA: Sage. p. 358.

18. Paustian-Underdahl, S. C., Walker , L. S., & Woehl, D. J. (2014, April 28). Gender and perceptions of leadership effectiveness: A meta-analysis of contextual moderators. Journal of Applied Psychology. Advance online publication. 1131-1140 http://dx.doi.org/10.1037/a0036751, pp. 1131-1140

19. Barbuto, J. E., Fritz, S. M., Matkin, G. S. & Marx, D. B. (2007, January), Effects of gender education, and age upon leaders' use of influence tactics and full range leadership behaviors. Sex Roles, 56, 71–83;

20. Van Engen, M. L., Van der Leeden, R., & Willemsen, T. M. (2010). *Gender from, context and leadership styles: A field study.* First published: 16 December 2010. https://doi.org/10.1348/096317901167532

21. Northouse, P. G. (2013). Leadership: Theory and Practice. Sixth edition. Los Angeles, CA: Sage. p. 350.

22. Palmer, P. (1990). *Leading within: Reflections on spirituality and leadership* .Campus Ministries: Indiana. p. 7.

23. Ludeman, K., & Erlandson, E. The Alpha Male Syndrome Synopsis. Worth Ethic Corporation. http://www.worthethic.com/the-alpha-male-syndrome.html

24. Paustian-Underdahl, S. C., Walker , L. S., & Woehl, D. J. (2014, April 28). Gender and perceptions of leadership effectiveness: A meta-analysis of contextual moderators. Journal of Applied Psychology.

Advance online publication. 1131-1140 http://dx.doi.org/10.1037/a0036751, pp. 1131-1140

Chapter 11: Shades of Truth: Myths, Spins and Double Standards

1. Definition of perjury. (18 U.S.C. § 1621).

2. Edman, T. W. (2001). Lies, Damn Lies, and Misleading Advertising: The Role of Consumer Surveys in the Wake of Mead Johnson v. Abbott Labs, 43 Wm. & Mary L. Rev. 417

   https://scholarship.law.wm.edu/wmlr/vol43/iss1/11. See also, The Four colors of Lies. How we change what others think, feel, believe and do. http://changingminds.org/explanations/behaviors/lying/four_lies.htm, and **www.ftc.gov**

3. Definition of Truth. www.merriam-webster.com/dictionary/truth

4. Pilate's question 'What is Truth?' John 18:38 NKJV

5. Taylor, C. (1992). *The Ethics of Authenticity*. Canadian Broadcasting Corporation. Sire, (2009). *The universe next door: A basic worldview catalog*. 5th ed. Chicago, IL: Intervarsity Press. www.ivpbooks.com. p. 220

6. Sire, J. W. (2009). *The universe next door: A basic worldview catalog*. 5th ed. Chicago, IL: Intervarsity Press. www.ivpbooks.com. On power, meta-narratives, and truth. pp. 221-225.

7. Nietszche, F. (1969). Beyond good and evil, sec. 54. In W. Kaufman. Ed. *The basic writings of Nietszche*. New York: Modern Library. On erosion of horizons.

8. Sire, J. W. (2009). The universe next door: A basic worldview catalog. 5th ed. Chicago, IL: Intervarsity Press. www.ivpbooks.com. On power, meta-narratives, and truth. p. 225

9. Sire, J. W. (2009). p. 221

10. Taylor, C. (1992). *Ethics of Authenticity*. Canadian Broadcasting Corporation. And Sire, (2009), p. 215: The consequences to cultures that have lost or removed the horizons of their culture, and by extension their identity their direction and world.

11. Associated Press. (2015, November 3). Betrayed by the Badge. The Mercury News. https://www.mercurynews.com/2015/11/03/betrayed-by-the-badge-hundreds-of-police-officers-across-the-u-s-lose-licenses-over-sex-misconduct/

12. Definitions of epistemology and ontology, and the differences between the two terms. The DifferenceBetween.net. http://www.differencebetween.net/science/health/difference-between-ontology-and-epistemology/

13. Friedman, T. L. (2007). *The World Is Flat 3.0: A Brief History of the Twenty-first Century*. Picador. New York, NY: Pan Books Ltd

14. Truth in lending Regulation Z. National Archives. Federal Register. The Daily Journal of the United States Government. https://www.federalregister.gov/truth-in-lending-regulation-z-

15. Hoyt, K. (2013). Women's Leadership. In P. Northouse. Leadership: Theory and Practice. p. 303, 357

16. Cuddy A. J. C. & Baily W. E. For working moms: How race and work status affect judgment of mothers. Backlash and the Double-Bind. http://www.hbs.edu/faculty/conferences/2013-w50-research-symposium/Documentss/cuddy.pdf   See also Evans & Breinig Chun, (2007), Shyns & Sanders, 2005; Sinclair, 2005, and negative reactions and social costs of women leaders.

17. Ayman, R., Korabik, K., & Morris, S. (2009). Is transformational leadership always perceived as effective? Male subordinates' devaluation of female transformational leaders. *Journal of Applied Social Psychology*, 39(4), 852-879. http://dx.doi.org/10.1111/j.1559-1816.2009.00463.x Also see Van Engen, M. L., Van der Leeden, R.,

& Willemsen, T. M. (2010). Gender, context and leadership styles: A field study. First published: 16 December 2010. https://doi.org/10.1348/096317901167532

18. Eagly, A. H., & Johnson, B. T. (1990). Gender and leadership style: A meta-analysis. *Psychological Bulletin*, 108, 233-256. p. 248.

19. US Census 2011; National Center for Education Statistics, "Table 318.30: Bachelor's, Master's, and Doctor's Degrees Conferred by Postsecondary Institutions, by Sex of Student and Discipline Division: 2013-14" 2015 Digest of Education Statistics (2015).

20. Tomlin, C. (1999). Black language style in sacred and secular contexts. New York: Caribbean Diaspora Press, Inc. p. 40, citing Smith, 1983.

21. Schultz, T. P. (1993). The economics of women's schooling. In J. Ker Conway, & S. C. Bourque (Eds.). The politics of women's education: Perspectives from Asia, Africa, and Latin America. (pp. 237 – 244). Ann Arbor, MI: The University of Michigan Press. p. 242

22. Gaslighting. https://www.theguardian.com/commentisfree/2016/apr/05/the-archers-domestic-abuse-gaslighting-sanity-abusive-relationship.

23. Sire, J. W. (2009). The universe next door: A basic worldview catalog. 5th ed. Chicago, IL: Intervarsity Press. www.ivpbooks.com. p. 216. Group as bound by the binding power of narratives.

24. McNeish, H. (2016). Malawi's fearsome chief, terminator of child-marriages. *Al Jazeera.* https://www.aljazeera.com/indepth/features/2016/03/malawi-fearsome-chief-terminator-child-marriages-160316081809603.html

25. Duster, A. M. (1970). *Crusade for Justice: The Autobiography of Ida B. Wells.* Chicago: University of Chicago Press.

Chapter 12: Metaphors For Framing Women's Leadership Experiences

1. The Loud noise when a bullet is fired. https://www.scienceabc. com/eyeopeners/why-is-there-such-a-loud-noise-when-a-bullet-is-fired.html

2. Harriet Tubman Quotes. (n.d.). BrainyQuote.com. Retrieved December 7, 2018, from BrainyQuote.com Web site: https://www. brainyquote.com/quotes/harriet_tubman_629149

3. Eagly & Carli in 2007 (https://hbr.org/2007/09/women-and-the-labyrinth-of-leadership

4. Hoyt, K. (2013). Women and Leadership. In P. Northous. Leadership Theory and Practice. p. 359.

5. Groeger, L. V. (2012, Nov. 15). Pipelines Explained: How Safe are America's 2.5 Million Miles of Pipelines? *ProPublica*. https://www. propublica.org/article/pipelines-explained-how-safe-are-americas-2.5-million-miles-of-pipelines

6. Fels, A. (2004). "Do women lack ambition?" Harvard Business Review. On Point. 9424, 2-11.

7. Olsson, S., & Walker, R. (2004)""Two wo-men and the boys": Patterns of identification and differentiation in senior women executives' representations of career identity." *Women in Management Review*. Women's Interest Module. 19, no. 5/6, 244 –251. p. 244

8. Lampe A. C. (2001). Book Reviews. *Gender, Work and Organization* 8(3), 346–351. p. 346

9. Cilizza, C. (2013, June 13). Hillary Clinton: 18 Million Cracks and the power of making History. Washington Post.

10. Kephart, P., and Schumacher, L. (2005 September 1). Has the 'Glass Ceiling' Cracked? An Exploration of Women Entrepreneurship. *Journal of Leadership and Organizational Studies*. https://journals. sagepub.com/doi/abs/10.1177/107179190501200102

11. Vargas, T. (2018, March 1). She coined the term 'glass ceiling'. She fears it will outlive her. Washington Post. https://www.washingtonpost.com/news/retropolis/wp/2018/03/01/she-coined-the-phrase-glass-ceiling-she-didnt-expect-it-to-outlive her/?noredirect=on&utm_term=.2f270bb0c531

12. Bruckmuller and Branscombe (2011) How women end up on the glass cliff. *Harvard Business Review.* https://hbr.org/2011/01/how-women-end-up-on-the-glass-cliff?referral=03758&cm_vc=rr_item_page.top_right. p. 433.

13. Hirschfeld Davis, J.(2018, Nov. 18). If not Pelosi, who should lead? The Question Hovers Over a Simmering Rebellion. *New York Times.* https://www.nytimes.com/2018/11/18/us/politics/nancy-pelosi-house-speaker-challenge.html

14. Songwriters: DON SCHLITZ The Gambler lyrics © Sony/ATV Music Publishing LLC

15. Senge, P. M. (2006). *The Fifth Discipline: The Art & Practice of the Learning Organization.* New York, NY: Doubleday, a division of Random House, Inc.

16. Ladkin, D. (2013, July 22,). From perception to flesh: A phenomenological account of the felt experience of leadership. *Leadership.* Sage Publications. https://journals.sagepub.com. https://doi.org/10.1177/1742715013485854

17. Bordo, S. (1993/2004). *Unbearable Weight: Feminism, Western Culture, and the Body.* Berkeley, CA: University of California Press.

18. Assael, H. *Consumer Behavior: A Strategic Approach.* New York, NY: New York University.

19. Portes, D. (2017, Jan. 5). Selective perception & Leadership. BizTimes. *Telegraph Herald.* https://www.telegraphherald.com/biztimes/articles/article_446d3feb-d2da-5140-9fbd-a264b6490348.html.

20. Latham, G. P. (2007). *Work Motivation: History, theory, research and practice.* Foundations for Organizational Science. Thousand Oaks: Sage Publications.

Chapter 13: Igniting A Revolution: A Case Study

1. Arendt, H. (1998). *The human condition.* Introduction by Margaret Canovan. Second edition. Chicago, Il; University of Chicago Press.

2. Cilizza, C. (2008). Hillary Clinton, 18 million cracks and the power of making history. The Fix-WP. Retrieved from: http://www.washingtonpost.com/blogs/the-fix/wp2013/06/13/hillary-clinton-18-million-cracks-and-the-power-of-making-history/?wprss=rss_politics@clsrd

3. Nanton, C. R. (2015). Shaping Leadership Culture: The Role of Adult Education in Developing and Sustaining the Next Generation of Women Leaders. In J. K. Holtz, S. B. Springer, C. J Boden-McGill. *Building Sustainable Futures for Adult Learners.* North Carolina: Information Age Publishing Inc. pp. 421-446.

4. www.dictionary.com. Definitions of a Revolution.

5. The Electoral College. https://www.factcheck.org/2008/02/the-reason-for-the-electoral-college/ and Hamilton, A. (1788). Federalist No. 68 The Mode of Electing the President. From the New York Packet. para 2, 3.

6. Gannon, M. J. (2001) *Cultural Metaphors: Readings, Research Translations, and Commentary.* 1st edition. Sage

7. Trompenaars, F., & Hampden-Turner, C. (2012). Riding the waves of culture: understanding diversity in global business. Revised and updated, third edition. New York: McGraw Hill. pp. 258

8. Warner, J. (2015). The women's leadership gap: Women's leadership by the numbers. https://www.americanprogress.org/issues/women/reports/2015/08/04/118743/the-womens-leadership-gap/

9. Bump P. (2016). Stronger Together. Campaign slogan. The Fix. *Washington Post.* https://www.washingtonpost.com/news/the-fix/wp/2016/10/19/hillary-clintons-84-proposed-campaign-slogans-ranked/ https://presidentsusa.net/campaignslogans.html

10. Texas Just Voted to Erase Hillary Clinton From the History Bookshttps://www.politicususa.com/2018/09/15/texas-just-voted-to-erase-hillary-clinton-from-the-history-books.html

11. DeSilver D (2018). A record number of women will be serving in the new Congress. Fact Tank News in Numbers. Pew Research Center. https://www.pewresearch.org/fact-tank/2018/12/18/record-number-women-in-congress/

12. Frost, R. (1932). The Road Not Taken. *The Poetry of Robert Frost* **by Robert Frost, edited by Edward Connery** Lathem.

13. Tavanti, M. & Werhane, P. H. (2013). On complacency, corporate cliffs, and power distance: global leadership ethics from ender and cultural studies perspectives. *Leadership and the Humanities.* V1, No.1, 22-30.

14. Greenleaf, R. K. (2002). *Servant Leadership: A Journey into the Nature of Legitimate Power and Greatness.* 25th Anniversary Edition. Robert K. Greenleaf Center.

Chapter 14: Honoring Your Hard-Wire

1. 2019 State of Women-owned Businesses: A Summary of important trends. Commissioned by American Express. https://www.nawbo.org/sites/nawbo/files/2014_state_of_women-owned_businesses.pdf See also, 2014 the 2014 State of Women-owned Businesses report.

2. BusinessWire (2017). Number of Women-Owned Businesses Growing 2.5 Times Faster Than National Average. https://markets.businessinsider.com/news/stocks/number-of-women-

owned-businesses-growing-2-5-times-faster-than-national-average-1007300927

3. Haimerl, A. (June 29, 2015) The fastest-growing group of entrepreneurs in America. Fortune. http://fortune.com/2015/06/29/black-women-entrepreneurs/. League of Black Women. Black Women and Risk http://events.leagueofblackwomen.org/wp-content/uploads/2011/05/Risk-and-Reward-Report1.pdf. See also, Weldon, M. article, No One Looks Like me. https://medium.com/@micheleweldon/no-one-looks-like-me-why-we-need-more-women-of-color-in-leadership-43f7621a2443

4. Williamson, M. (1992). A Return To Love: Reflections on the Principles of A Course in Miracles. New York: Harper Collins. pp. 190.

5. Texas Just Voted to Erase Hillary Clinton From the History Bookshttps://www.politicususa.com/2018/09/15/texas-just-voted-to-erase-hillary-clinton-from-the-history-books.html

6. Marian Wright Edelman Quotes. (n.d.). BrainyQuote.com. https://www.brainyquote.com/quotes/marian_wright_edelman_158752

7. Warner, J. & Corley, D. (2017, May 21). The Women's Leadership Gap. Women's Leadership by the numbers.https://www.americanprogress.org/issues/women/reports/2017/05/21/432758/womens-leadership-gap/

8. Tyler Scott, K. (2017). Interview, *In the Lead*.

9. Senge, P. M. (2006). The Fifth Discipline: The Art & Practice of the Learning Organization. New York, NY: Doubleday, a division of Random House, Inc.

10. Bump P. (2016). Stronger Together. Campaign slogan. The Fix. Washington Post. https://www.washingtonpost.com/news/the-fix/wp/2016/10/19/hillary-clintons-84-proposed-campaign-slogans-ranked/ https://presidentsusa.net/campaignslogans.html.

11. Kotter, J. P. (2012). *Leading Change*. Boston: Harvard Business Review Press.

www.ingramcontent.com/pod-product-compliance
Lightning Source LLC
Chambersburg PA
CBHW061309220326
41599CB00026B/4795